Praise for
EXPERIENCING GOD

"*Experience of God* is what people need, want, and find in these examples from the life of one of my favorite saints. I love how Jon starts with 'Freeing captive creatures' and finishes with 'Receiving motherly love,' always with close attention to the sources."

—**James Martin, SJ**, author of *Come Forth: The Promise of Jesus's Greatest Miracle*

"*Experiencing God* is an uplifting and deeply grounding invitation to encounter the Divine as Saint Francis did—through the simple, embodied, and radical acts of everyday life. Francis teaches us that the everyday, incarnate world matters, that the sacred is found in birdsong, in surrendering worldly power and comforts, and in loving those cast aside. With warmth and insight, Sweeney helps us feel close to St. Francis and shows how Francis' way of living—joyfully unattached yet profoundly rooted—offers us an antidote to the anxiety of our times. This book is a gift to all who long to experience God not in some distant heaven, but here, in the fullness of today."

—**Kaira Jewel Lingo**, Buddhist teacher, author of *We Were Made for These Times*; co-author of *Healing Our Way Home: Black Buddhist Teachings on Ancestors, Joy, and Liberation*

"With great passion and skill, Sweeney invites a broad readership to explore the poetic, mystical, and social insights of this venerated medieval figure. This volume offers the contemporary reader the opportunity to commune with St. Francis across space and time."

—**Rabbi Or N. Rose**, founding Director of the Betty Ann Greenbaum Miller Center for Interreligious Learning & Leadership at Hebrew College; author of *My Legs Were Praying: A Biography of Abraham Joshua Heschel*

"I can give you one hundred reasons to read *Experiencing God: 36 Ways According to Saint Francis of Assisi*. The wisdom shared transcends centuries and is a roadmap for living today. From living in the present, praying alone in the woods, singing and dancing, overcoming fear, and turning emotions into actions, this holy masterpiece is one of Jon Sweeney's best. It has given me a friend in Saint Francis for a lifetime. A divine encounter."

—**Karen Kiefer**, Director, The Church in the 21st Century Center, Boston College

EXPERIENCING GOD

“One might say salvation means exactly this sort of holy wind-swept freedom—or that salvation *should* be like this.”

DRAWING BY THOMAS SKOWRON, OFM CAP

EXPERIENCING GOD

36 WAYS ACCORDING TO SAINT FRANCIS OF ASSISI

JON M. SWEENEY

BOOK PUBLISHING COMPANY
RHINEBECK, NEW YORK

Paperback ISBN 9781966608059
eBook ISBN 9781966608066

Library of Congress Cataloging-in-Publication Data

Names: Sweeney, Jon M., 1967- author
Title: Experiencing God : 36 ways according to Saint Francis of Assisi / Jon M. Sweeney.
Description: Rhinebeck, New York : Monkfish Book Publishing Company, [2026] | Includes bibliographical references.
Identifiers: LCCN 2025032209 (print) | LCCN 2025032210 (ebook) | ISBN 9781966608059 paperback | ISBN 9781966608066 ebook
Subjects: LCSH: Francis, of Assisi, Saint, 1182-1226 | Mysticism--Catholic Church | Spiritual life--Catholic Church | Spiritual exercises
Classification: LCC BX4700.F6 S9146 2026 (print) | LCC BX4700.F6 (ebook)
LC record available at https://lccn.loc.gov/2025032209
LC ebook record available at https://lccn.loc.gov/2025032210

Book and cover design by Colin Rolfe

Monkfish Book Publishing Company
22 East Market Street, Suite 304
Rhinebeck, New York 12572
(845) 876-4861
monkfishpublishing.com

FOR ALL OF US, WITH HOPE

Contents

Before We Get Started

Let's be real, this book publishes in a precarious time. The world is again caught up in fascism and abuses of power. Appeals to justice and the common good seem unable to provide a sufficient check or balance. Idealism is being rapidly abandoned. We're occasionally reminded by well-meaning people to keep hope alive (I heard Dr. King's biographer, Jonathan Eig, do so at a recent book festival), which leads to some unavoidable questions. Are appeals to God in this moment naïve, at best, and escapist, at worst? Is experiencing God's presence even possible? Am I ridiculous to suggest that we try, let alone look to someone from 800 years ago for examples of how? For that matter, was the experience of God *ever* real?

I think it is possible and it's important, because when humanity is in darkness and civilization can't be counted upon, we remember what preceded both. As for escapism, those charges usually come from people for whom the world as it is is basically fine; the world has a hold on them (as it does most of us) and so far, it's been working out okay.

This was true for Francis Bernardone (that's the birth name of Francis of Assisi), too. Until it wasn't. And then he began teaching everyone who would listen that we are in fact slaves to money and power and persona; the world has made sure of that. But if you listen, he'll show a way to escape—in order to save your life.

This book is about this Francis—the world's most popular saint, back when we used to keep track of such things—and how he experienced God. And there's no theology here. This is simply how Francis experienced the sacred. He lived in turbulent times like our own, when men (I use the word deliberately) were terrible to each other. And what you have here is a series of honest-to-God ways of experiencing God inspired by Francis' life and practices.

It was 1226, exactly 800 years ago when he died in the Umbrian hill-town his name made famous. If you've ever had the opportunity to be there as the sun sets, you've seen the basilicas named for him and his friend Clare radiating with pink, beige, and orange gleams of Mount Subasio limestone. They face each other from the two ends of town. Francis' life was colorful like those stones, and we're fortunate to have accurate accounts of where he went, and why, and what he did and said.

Why go all the way back to Saint Francis for these experiences of God? Because he's respected by people of all religious backgrounds, and by people who want nothing to do with religion. Whether you're involved in religious organizations or not, we all want a connection to the sacred and the holy. We just call it by different names. I have None (no official religious affiliation) and Done (officially done with religion) friends who love Francis of Assisi. I have Jewish friends, Muslim friends, Buddhist friends, and Hindu friends who claim Francis as their own. So many times, a new friend has remarked to me, "He's my favorite saint!" to my reply, "Really?!" This is because when you get down to the essentials of Francis' spirituality, you find water that flows also from the wells of other great traditions.

There's no question Francis felt God's presence. Some of these are embodied ways. Some have a more internal expression of piety. Some are acts of justice. Others are passionate expressions of belief that, Francis tells us, were how he knew divine company.

We have abundant documentation of who Francis was, what he said, and what he did. He wrote a thin volume's-worth of writings himself, and he had many brother friars and associates left after he died to recount stories. Yet, in what I choose to retell here, I'll be following an important dictum: "There is no use in writing of things past unless they can be made in fact things present."[1]

I leave out a few things on purpose: for example, the miracle placed upon him that seems to separate him from everyone else: the stigmata—perhaps you've heard about that one—a replication of Christ's wounds on Francis' hands, feet, and side. One doesn't exactly go out and imitate a stigmata, unless you're certifiable. I leave it out also mostly because Francis never spoke of it, not once. Perhaps he believed that some things are not to be talked about. It's like what poet Fanny Howe has said: "The evidence of a successful miracle is the return of hunger."[2]

Also, if you study the life of Francis, you discover that there are plenty of things he does and instructs others to also do that aren't ways of experiencing God, but are instead something else. We know for instance that he would roll in the snow when feelings of lust came upon him. He said that the bitter cold would put out the fire inside him. That's an interesting act of penitence, but not a way he experienced God's presence. These other practices are also sometimes done out of duty and reverence, such as sweeping churches clean, rebuilding stone walls, or generally working with his hands every day, which Francis required of every friar, to demonstrate that everyone must do their share. So in contrast to works of penitence, duty, or reverence—what one early biographer, Bonaventure, calls "obedience laid upon him'"*—what follows here are thirty-six ways to find love and joy by connecting with the Creator, Lover, and Friend.

There's one more reason why people all over the world, from every way of life, seem drawn to Francis. He's special among the world's famous spiritual teachers in that he only seemed to be certain of two things: the necessity of asking questions, and the frequency of his own faults. He asks questions again and again, sometimes interrogating himself, "Who are you, God? And who am I?" (See way of experiencing God #12, for this.) And he accuses himself of hypocrisy, of showing off, of performing his piety, over and over too. (There's no example of this in the book, so just take my word for it.) That's why we trust him. You never ever ever feel like Francis is trying to sell you something.

Early last century the English writer Evelyn Underhill published the world's most popular book on mysticism. She defined mysticism as "experience in its most intense form"—a phrase that's often been repeated.[3] I think she overstates the point unless *whenever* we have an intense experience it is mystical. For example, I've heard (and witnessed) how giving birth to a child is way up there on the list of most intense experiences possible. So is sex, or at least it can be. And falling in love—can be too. Near-death experiences are more intense than anything else in life, for many. Perhaps, too, the death of someone very close to us. To experience transcendence, divine imminence, amazing grace, a surpassing love, in ordinary life in ways that match these sorts of human experiences is what this book about Saint Francis is also about.

All thirty-six experiences can absolutely be replicated in life today, wherever you find yourself. Each is a simple means of God-connection. They are not modes of thinking. They can be performed, carried out. The five senses are alive as we do them.

* BO, 2.7. See "A Guide to Sources" on the next page.

Francis wasn't so special that he believed or acted as if he had spiritually "arrived." I like how Julie Seido Nelson, a Buddhist teacher from Boston, recently put this in a Zen context: "[E]nlightenment is not a matter of one and done. The possibility of awakening is in every moment."[4] For Francis too. There's not a single experience of God here that is in any way closed off from you or me or anyone else looking for connections with the holy that, if we aren't paying attention, can escape us for days, decades, or a lifetime. Don't let that happen. Try looking to Saint Francis for guidance. People have been doing so for 800 years and counting.

A final note. Why are there thirty-six, exactly? There's no clever reason. That's the number of ways of experiencing God I found when I did my investigation, pouring again over the earliest biographies and historical collections of anecdotes written about Francis.

A Guide to Sources

At the end of each chapter are sources listed where you can go to find accounts in their original form. The following abbreviations are used in pointing to those thirteenth and fourteenth century originals.

There are many English editions of these texts. Franciscans and scholars these days usually turn to the four big volumes called *Francis of Assisi: Early Documents*, published by New City Press (1999-2020). A generation earlier and it was the single volume *St. Francis of Assisi, Writings and Early Biographies: English Omnibus of Sources*, published by Franciscan Herald Press (1983). There is also the edition that I produced some years ago: *The Complete Francis of Assisi* (Paraclete Press, 2015), which is often used by Secular and Third Order Franciscans.

AC	The Assisi Compilation
AP	Anonymous of Perugia
BML	Bonaventure's Minor Legend
BO	Bonaventure's Major Life
DF	The Deeds of Blessed Francis and His Companions
FW	Francis' own writings (taken from *The Complete Francis of Assisi*, referring to page numbers in that book)
JS	The Life of Saint Francis, by Julian of Speyer
LT	Legend of Three Companions

LF	*The Little Flowers of Saint Francis* (for numbering of these stories I follow the chronological organization in *The Complete Francis of Assisi*).
MP	Mirror of Perfection (Lemmens edition)
TC	Thomas of Celano, First Life
TS	Thomas of Celano, Second Life (aka *The Remembrance of the Desire of a Soul*)

All the translations from these sources used in this book are similar to those found in the various common editions in English, but I haven't kept to a single one. Most quotations are my own renderings.

THE 36 WAYS

1 Freeing captive creatures

In one of his most iconic gestures, Francis set creatures free, feeling God's joy in doing so. Most people wouldn't think of doing this. We tend more often to hold things close.

I live lovingly with a dog and two cats, and I feed the birds from my porch most of the year, knowing full well that I do so for me more than them; they have many natural sources of food and have done fine without my assistance for millions of years. I do it to keep them close.

When Francis was drawn to animals, birds, and creatures—which he was all his life—he was also uncomfortable "catching" them, holding them, or keeping them in cages. He seems to have understood their need and desire to be free, and he seems to have identified with their instinct to spread their wings or legs and go.

A worm's bristles help it move through the soil, and moving through the soil in this way is what a worm is meant to do. The hind legs of a rabbit are so strong that a rabbit can go from standstill to full scamper in half a second. A fish's tail fin moves it quickly through water, and its other fins help steer where the fish needs to go. When a fish does this, and swims freely in a moving stream, it is an example of the original beauty of a creature.

I wonder how Francis must have pondered the wildness, the instinctual Creator-lovingness of human beings who also want to be free, when he was insisting on setting loose non-human creatures who had been caught. Books, in fact, could be written about all the human institutions the saint of Assisi himself steered clear of, so intent was he on being free like a bird.

There was the time when a fisherman took Francis out in his boat. When he reeled in his best catch of the day, he handed it to the friar, grateful to be able to provide for him and thank him. Francis received the fish in his hands, blessed it, and tossed it back into the water, watching the fish swim rapidly away.

He wasn't always silent when doing these things. With birds—whom he seemed most often to be setting free—Francis always appeared to want to communicate with words, saying things like, "Sisters, don't let yourselves be captured. Fly free, as you were made to do! Sing and praise your Creator now, because that makes God happy." In some religions, angels might be disguised as birds. How many a child, seeing a hummingbird for the first time, has believed this! In one beautiful Islamic legend (Attar's *Conference of the Birds*), birds are even seen speaking the words of God, and in a Tibetan Buddhist legend a cuckoo preaches dharma to fellow avians (see *Buddha's Law Among the Birds*).

Francis would stop by the outdoor market in Assisi where boys and girls and other working people were selling doves. Picture a warm weekday morning and vendors all around, their wares displayed in carts that they wheeled to that place. In Umbria in the year 1206 or 1207, doves were used for dinner, and also as egg-layers. They sat noisily in their cages that morning, cooing, talking with each other and the open air.

To readers of the Bible, a dove sometimes symbolizes God's Spirit, because the Gospel of Matthew says that when Jesus was baptized in the Jordan River, God in the guise of a dove alighted on Jesus' shoulder at precisely that moment. This is why, in fine art, you'll often see a dove in a painting, symbolizing the creative spirit of God hovering over a special scene, as if to breathe life into things, or inspire fresh perspectives.

On this occasion, Francis convinced a boy with cages full of beautiful white, gray, black, and brown doves to give two to him. He then turned to one side and, throwing his arms in the air, let them fly. There is also an anecdote of Francis saving a rabbit from a similar fate. It was caught by someone in a trap but the saint took and carried it to the woods, where he set it down in the grass, watching it go. His curiosity was fired by his gentleness, and then he wanted everyone to be free.

I can only imagine how onlookers must have thought Francis was out of his mind. Who does this?! *Here's that Bernardone kid again. He really has gone mad.* But a counter-cultural sort of foolishness was part of Francis' makeup, and part of why his spiritual movement caught fire soon after this.

I feel I can see Francis' imagination at that moment, flying with those birds, free of constraints, or scampering with that rabbit into the undercover—leaving behind the worldly expectations of his earthly father, and all the condemnations of people who knew him before his conversion and made fun of him—soaring into the sky or running fast, with pleasure and joy. I'm no theologian, but one might say salvation means exactly this sort of holy wind-swept freedom—or that salvation *should* be like this. Spanish liberation theologian Jon Sobrino has said, "In Jesus' eyes God's ultimate historical word is love, whereas the ultimate historical word of power in the human world is oppression."[5]

Francis did the same thing with sheep and lambs, often begging those who were about to prepare them for a meal to let him instead set them back on their feet. However, there was one instance when a lamb was gifted to Francis and he was comfortable keeping it. Monks and friars were usually not supposed to keep pets, because care for a pet in a monastery or friary, or in any living-in-community situation, can become a point of division and that's to be avoided as much as possible. (This is still true in most places.) Also, it usually costs money to care for an animal, and Francis' vow was to poverty. But most of all, he loved to see animals roaming free.

So Francis tried to set the lamb free, but the lamb had already grown attached to him and followed closely at his heels all around the friary. It was often heard bleating as it trailed Francis around the little chapel below Assisi called Portiuncula.* Finally, the friar entrusted this lamb with a friend named Jacopa, and she cared for it in the ways that a shepherd would. She also wove some of its wool with which she lined Francis' simple habit one winter when he was sick and needed to avoid the cold.

There were other shepherds who remembered Francis speaking to their flocks as they were grazing and he was walking by, and the sheep responding to him as if to a good friend. The creatures "focused on him and gave him such a loud bleating that the shepherds were shocked at how they frisked about him so extraordinarily," one account says.

His experience of loving, caring for, and especially freeing captive creatures was a way of experiencing the joy and pleasure of God, who wants to set all captives free. It wasn't simply that doves and lambs symbolized God to Francis. (He was often remembering in his sermons how Christ was compared to a lamb.) One couldn't say the same, surely, about worms and fish? Loving the captive creature—and helping to literally set it free—is what this expression of Francis was about, and it was that freedom in the air or water or grass that meant feeling God's presence.

* From an Italian word meaning "little portion." Similarly, a name Francis used for himself was "Poverello," meaning "little poor man."

Would it do the same for you, if you found a creature to care for, or to even set free? I think you should try.

—

Find the story: LF 20, TC 61, BO 8.7
Consider a scripture: "The spirit of the Lord GOD is upon me because the LORD has anointed me; he has sent me to bring good news to the oppressed, to bind up the brokenhearted, to proclaim liberty to the captives and release to the prisoners." (Isaiah 61:1)

And from liberation theologian Jon Sobrino: "[Hope] grows out of reconciliation, forgiveness, the immense reserve of primordial saintliness that exists in the Third World. And it grows out of the solidarity of people and groups who live in the world of abundance but have never given in to its logic; who have instead found life by trying to give life to the victims of this world. These are small gestures, but they help to set history back on course."[6]

2 Praying alone in the woods

There are simple reasons why walking outdoors is good for you. Studies show that walking among trees, with birds and creatures about, undergrowth of flowers and tall grasses will make you healthier and happier. Oxygen levels are higher among an abundance of plants. Stress hormone levels of cortisol and adrenaline go down as you pad your way on natural paths. Even fifteen minutes a day in the woods is shown to boost antioxidants and improve your immunity for fighting disease. So, for God's sake, for your own sake, go for a walk in the trees and fields whenever you can.

Walking in the woods will also help open your soul, say the mystics and saints of nearly every tradition. Imagine your soul as a physical shape, pulsating like a human lung, throbbing, expanding, and contracting more effectively as the oxygen-filled space of the woods increases your soul cavity on a natural walk. The *Grund*, or "ground," of your soul is the same *Grund* that is God, said Meister Eckhart, and that ground is in fact groundless. That's a Christian koan if I've ever heard one! In any case, cramped quarters or city strolling won't fill your soul with oxygen like the woods can. This is why many human rights charters declare that access to nature is a basic human right.

Francis didn't need medical studies or charters to understand this. I'm not sure he even needed the scriptures of his tradition. He knew it firsthand, from personal experience, from many, many walks in the woods. Henry David Thoreau was Francis' spiritual descendant in this regard. Thoreau wrote one day to his journal after a woods walk: "The strains of the Aeolian harp and of the wood thrush are the truest and loftiest preachers that I know now left on this earth. I know of no missionaries to us heathen comparable to them. They, as it were, lift us up in spite of ourselves. They intoxicate, they charm us.... I would be drunk, drunk, drunk, dead drunk to this world with it forever. He that hath ears, let him hear."[7]

And Francis met God there. He knew the connection between the woods and the ground of his soul from what happened to him, in him, in the woods. That's what religious experience is about. We often see Francis going apart from his spiritual brothers, or with just one or two of them tagging along, to a remote place of rest and retreat. He was as active as anyone, doing physical work to help the collective, and aiding people in tangible ways, but he clearly became exhausted too and needed regular doses of quiet woods time by himself.

It's almost unnatural to picture Francis sitting inside. I'm not sure he ever sat in a chair or reclined on a couch. Similarly, he didn't ponder birds in nests (as Vincent Van Gogh famously did), but rather, birds escaping cages. You'll find museum paintings of Francis seated at a desk, contemplating a skull in the way that artists often imagined saints doing, but that's not who he really was. He was almost always in one of two places: a church (preferably an abandoned one), or outdoors. And when he went to pray alone it was most often into the woods.

In the first source listed below, it is his friar friends Masseo and Elias who are named as his companions. But at the forest edge, Francis quickly leaves them behind to go alone to pray. At this point, what we know about what happened next is due to the fact that Masseo and Elias were spying on their teacher—probably from behind the oleander and chickory bushes in those woods around Assisi. Francis' friends were often doing this—secretly watching him—which is a bit weird and voyeuristic, but if they hadn't we might not know as much about where he went and what he did.

The alone part is essential here too. "He would seek lonely places," as Bonaventure puts it, suggesting that maybe the woods themselves were incidental. There are plenty of "lonely places" in the world. On other occasions, Francis prayed alone in small caves, which were found all over one side of Mount Subasio, which rises above Assisi. But to get there, Francis still had to leave the city, follow the path across open fields and to the woods, and then hike up Subasio, which was home to the flowering ash, the porcupine, and the rock partridge.

To see this expanse today you only have to visit Assisi and wander the twelve acres of trails set aside by Italy's National Heritage Trust behind the Basilica of Saint Francis. This is lovely to do, but it has changed a lot over eight centuries. Neatly cultivated today, it was then rugged, "lonely," as Bonaventure said, and often the hangout of people who felt cast away from good society. (It is one of the ironies of our strange saint that it's probably because of the presence of unwanted people there that Francis felt so comfortable.)

During the time when his conversion to religious life was in its initial stages, he and another friend whose name we don't know would leave Assisi over and over in search of one particular cave. The journey would have taken them about an hour. And there, we're told, Francis would leave the friend at the cave's entrance so that he could go inside alone to pray.

He didn't mind the dangerous vibe of the woods or the caves. We have stories of him alone facing criminals on forest paths. For this reason, there must have been times when no one wanted to follow him. On one occasion, in the middle of winter, snow had blanketed the ground; a group of rough men met him alone on the road, in song; and much annoyed by him, they tossed Francis into the ditch. The anecdote concludes with Francis waiting until the roughs have gone away and then jumping to his feet, singing and shouting with joy.

"He was burning inwardly with a divine fire," a biographer tells us, as to why Francis so often went to pray in the woods. And a "greatness of love was inspired in him" in such places.

I suggest that this is not so uncommon an experience. Much that Francis did was ordinary. At times, I think it is so simple that we believe it can't possibly be true. Will I feel God's presence if I take regular walks in the woods, listen to other creatures, pay attention to little more than my foot fall? Perhaps so. In those embodied ways, we can almost involuntarily pray. The praying happens in us like a heartbeat: you may not even be aware it's happening.

This has become such a common aspiration, since Francis, that when Mary Oliver writes "I was a bride married to amazement" in one of her most quoted poems, it becomes a not-so-secular scripture.[8] We are not trying to accomplish anything. These are the moments when, in the words of my friend Brother Paul Quenon, who has been a Trappist monk for nearly seventy years, we're living "the useless life"—and to the good. We are also, in the words of the ancient Chinese philosopher Laozi, "leaving the world be."

So leave your usual indoor spaces sometimes to expand your soul. This worked for Francis so well that he soon began to cancel plans to leave Assisi for adventure. He'd always been looking for where to go, and what to do. What's next. Maybe he thought he could save the world. But now he had so much he wanted to do right there, at home, or just a woods away.

—

Find the story: LF 19, 17, 3, 27; BO 1.5, 2.5
Consider a scripture: "Then Jesus went with them to a place called Gethsemane, and he said to his disciples, 'Sit here while I go over there and pray.'" (Matthew 26:36)

And consider the implications suggested here: "The world is a sacred vessel that cannot be changed. He who changes it will destroy it. He who seizes it will lose it." (Laozi, *Tao Te Ching*, chapter 29)

3 Allowing yourself to weep

We've all cried uncontrollably at one time or another. Hopefully. But isn't it interesting that what we know is good for us is often what we avoid doing most of all. Most often, we stop ourselves from crying. No one wants to be known as a blubberer. Cry for more than a second or two and you'll be accused of being unhinged, weak, immature.

People feel uncomfortable around us when we cry. It unsettles people. I remember when I was an executive in a publishing office, asking someone to go home for the day because they couldn't stop crying. "You're upsetting other people," I said that afternoon nearly thirty years ago, and Chandra, if you're out there reading this, I am sorry.

Physicians and psychologists sometimes say that if we bottle up our tears, we can end up no longer being able to cry at all. And sometimes being unable to cry is a sign of clinical depression—someone who needs to seek help. Other people wish they could weep and cannot.

We see Francis crying on many occasions, almost quickly, blubberingly, shamelessly. In fact, knowing nothing really about infection and disease, the early chroniclers attributed the blindness the saint experienced in his last few years to an "excess of weeping." Why all the tears? Towards the end, they were indeed a symptom of the glaucoma he suffered from; but before then they were manifestation of a tenderness that grew slowly inside him.

Before he ever left his father's house Francis began to hide from his dad, wanting to avoid his demands, his fists and wrath. We're told by the earliest biographer how Francis' father once organized a posse of friends and neighbors to search for the son who had attempted to steal from the dad in order to give money to the poor. For a month, Francis hid in a place that was known to only one other person. We aren't told who that person was—but we are told of the "flowing tears" that Francis "prayed," and that the saint paired his crying with fasting, like people used to do to deliberately make themselves weak in the expectation that God would eventually make them strong again.

You've heard (or maybe experienced) how crying, real weeping, can be cathartic? Endorphins are released by the brain, and these help to block nerve cells that receive pain signals. In other words, you feel better. Maybe this is why, despite being in that unpleasant hiding place, which was described as a "black pit," Francis' weeping and fasting led to feelings of "an indescribable happiness." Francis felt much better after his crying. It doesn't say that he heard a special response from God, only that he felt a happiness that could have come only from God.

Other experts—scientists who study biology and culture—suggest that weeping isn't cathartic so much as it is akin to prayer. As an infant weeps for its mother's response, so do we, perhaps, weep for our divine mother. One scientist calls this "the neural circuitry of crying," and a Catholic professor of Hebrew Bible explains, "Study of emotion generally and weeping in particular does not support the cathartic model. Weeping is a social behavior, and emotions are not like fluids."[9]

There are other stories of Francis in tears, and they are often a lament. He wept in sorrow, remembering the years of wasted time before he paid attention to God and others with his life. This kind of crying is countercultural today too for most Christians. We tend to believe that once we've established ourselves on the Christian path through words or sacraments of conversion and a life to match, that there is no more time for lamenting tears. One thinks of Augustine's mother Monica weeping for his soul *before* Augustine's conversion, who is told by her bishop that her boy, "the son of these tears," is no longer lost.

There is time for lament throughout life. For one thing, a heart trained in service to God is a heart that remains broken. Psalm 80—a song of lament, prayed by monks and friars in and out of convents, and by Jews and Christians for millennia—expresses this beautifully, giving language to a personal conversion of daily activity, with the metaphor of "turning," asking God to turn back toward us, and prompting ourselves to turn back to God.

We often go through long periods without a lament, and that may be because we don't allow ourselves to feel what's happening. We've become good at distractions. But both the psalmist and a good psychiatrist will tell you lament is good for your soul and your health. It is natural. *Not* lamenting is what's unnatural.

Francis was also known to weep when contemplating the Passion of Christ, both in chapel, and just walking around. In those days it was apparently common to cry out of what was called "piety and compassion." In our terms, this means being gentle-hearted.

Finally, lamenting never ends in this life when we're committed to living for others. How can we love without sometimes crying? All around us people are crying. One early fourteenth-century source called *The Tree of the Crucified Life of Jesus* puts it this way: "It was because Francis was aware of spending his days in a valley of tears that he was habitually weeping." Even better are these words from Black theologian Howard Thurman: "You must go through some things, crying all the way, perhaps, if you are ever to live with them without crying. This is an important law of living. There are many experiences which we face that are completely overwhelming. As we see them, they are too terrible even to contemplate. And yet we must face them and deal with them directly."[10]

—

Find the story: TC 10; LF 37, 31; LT 14
Consider a scripture: "God's Spirit is right alongside helping us along. If we don't know how or what to pray, it doesn't matter. He does our praying in and for us, making prayer out of our wordless sighs, our aching groans. He knows us far better than we know ourselves, knows our pregnant condition, and keeps us present before God. That's why we can be so sure that every detail in our lives of love for God is worked into something good." (Romans 8:26-28, The Message)

And how did Rumi put it? "You have to keep your heart breaking until it opens."

4 Practicing joy in small hardships

Say "Try practicing joy" to a friend today and you may hear back "Try going to hell." Anyone who suggests joy so casually must not understand what life is all about. A joy reflex might reveal someone dangerously out of touch with reality—or their neighbors, or their environment—making their comments irrelevant in terms of what heals the world or puts it back together. Reminds me of John Milton's Satan noticing Adam and Eve cuddling in the Garden of Eden and calling "hateful" those "imparadised in one another's arms" (*Paradise Lost*, IV:505-6)!

We know how that Garden of Eden joy turned out; their cuddling was a seventeenth-century version of Instagram posing. Looking for, identifying, posing, let alone "practicing" joy—is simply not real.

But that also isn't altogether true. I think of an essay by Robert Louis Stevenson from 1888 in which he criticized the novels of another writer who had created a brutal realism to correct the romanticism of an earlier era. Emile Zola used the gritty and grimy to try to "make it real," as my teenage daughter might say. Stevenson objected on the grounds that the "cheap desire and cheap fears" of Zola's characters, showing them immersed in "life's dullness and man's meanness," leaves out other truths. "The true realism, always and everywhere," Stevenson argued, "is that of the poets: to find out where joy resides, and give it a voice far beyond singing." Because joy *is* a part of life. Or it is meant to be. If you've subdued or misplaced it, perhaps it's time to start again.

It was one of those miserable days of cold rain in winter, as Francis and Brother Leo were walking home to St. Mary of the Angels, the little chapel in the valley below Assisi. On that muddy road, Francis called out to Leo, who was walking a bit ahead of him, "Leo, if our friars are an example of holiness and integrity everywhere in the world, doing everything exactly as they have been called to do, there is really no joy in that."

Leo said nothing, but kept walking. It was one of those cold rainy days of an Italian winter. Francis and Leo never wore the sort of shoes that would help someone make it through sticky mud. Leo wasn't haven't the best time.

Francis called out again—Leo was even further ahead now—saying, "If a friar could help the blind to see, or the dumb to speak, the source of joy isn't in any of that either!"

Again, Leo said nothing. It was raining harder. Maybe he didn't hear Francis. Maybe, on this one occasion, he didn't really care what his friend was trying to say.

This disconnection went on a few times more. Francis kept talking. "If we knew all there was to know in the world, there would be no joy in that either." And Leo kept ignoring him. Just shut up. Leo was wet and cold and irritable.

Francis was walking along as if it was a sunny Umbrian afternoon. It wasn't. He turned up the volume one more time, saying, "You know, if we could speak with the tongues of angels, and knew the courses of the stars, the source of joy isn't there."

Finally, Brother Leo turned around, soaked of clothes and angry in the face. He muttered, "Fine! Tell me. Where then is the source of joy to be found?"

Francis said: "When we arrive at St. Mary's, soaked and chilled and hungry, and if the brother on duty comes to the gate when we ring and says, 'Who are you? Go away' and leaves us outside in the wet cold night, and then we endure more insults, waiting there, and this goes on and on, and if we bear all of it with patience and charity in our hearts. That is the source of joy. Because we accept everything that's happening now in as much as we bear the sufferings of Jesus Christ. We do it because we love him."

The humor of this story is how it's suffused with Francis' personal contentment—even reveling in the cold wetness of a walk that would have been, for most anyone else, a lousy experience—without comment or agreement from Leo. It takes us a while to catch on to what's happening. Leo's early non-agreement is either frustration and exhaustion, or simply cluelessness.

There were also times when Francis was sick and he accepted that condition as a small hardship to learn from. At other times, domestic difficulties were met with an unusual patience. One of these was the presence of mice where he ate and slept. The fact that we know mice were there, "running around him, and even over him," shows that he minded these—or he would have minded it, if instead he didn't decide to bear the small hardship with a grin (maybe even joy?), as a small penance.

I recently wrote and helped perform a little one act play about Francis composing the "Canticle of the Creatures." This is the real situation where that experience with the mice originally took place. There are only two characters in my play and scene one begins with it. The part I played was Brother Leo, who acts as a kind of narrator speaking to the audience from the edge of the stage.

> In the garden of San Damiano, outside the walls of the convent where Sister Clare and the other professed women reside and pray, my Brother Francis lies on a cot, beneath a

> simple temporary shelter that has been prepared for him. Sick and frequently unwell, he is being cared for by Clare as his eyesight grows dimmer. In pain, he desires her presence now more than any other. Even me, and I'm his best friend, Brother Leo.
>
> In the valley below, Francis hears occasional voices, and the general business of the town. Most of the time he lies quietly, but not motionless.
>
> What happens next, some will say, was a temptation of the devil. It was "by divine permission that for increase of his affliction and his merit"—mice begin to infest his hut.

Then the stage light shines on Francis, speaking, and there's no one else around. He says: "There are so many mice in this cell of mine that they are running all over my body and all around me night and day. I cannot rest, or pray."

He continues, looking up the heavens: "Oh God, look on me and comfort me in these afflictions. Help me to endure them with patience." Just then, a mouse runs across his legs.

The point is, enduring small hardships was part of human life for Francis. He didn't really Christianize this the way that other saints have done so in more recent centuries. The attitude is more like *Tutto passa*, as the Italians say, "Everything passes." To take a different approach—God forbid, to imagine that you are going to always steer things your way—is to live untruthfully, with arrogance and self-importance, and without the gratitude that comes from acceptance of what is.

"Enjoy your problems," said Shunryu Suzuki Roshi, the Sōtō Zen monk and teacher who did more than anyone else to popularize Buddhism in the United States in the twentieth century. "To live is enough." That's the idea—and the practice.

—

Find the story: LF 30, AC 83
Consider a scripture: "My brothers and sisters, whenever you face various trials, consider it all joy, because you know that the testing of your faith produces endurance. And let endurance complete its work, so that you may be complete and whole, lacking in nothing." (James 1:2-4, NRSV)

And from part two, called "Right Attitude," of Suzuki Roshi's *Zen Mind, Beginner's Mind:* "We should appreciate what we are doing. There is no preparation for something else."[11]

5 Lifting hands and eyes to the sky

Example #2, "Praying alone in the woods," finds its expansion here. That way of experiencing God was mostly about the where. This is about the embodied how. In those woods and caves and elsewhere, Francis would lift his head and hands up to sky, which was, for him, the heavens. And why *wouldn't* he feel that way?

> The heavens declare the glory of God,
> and the skies announce what his hands have made.
> Day after day they tell the story; night after night
> they tell it again.
> They have no speech or words; they have no voice to
> be heard.
> But their message goes out through all the world.
> (Psalm 19:1-4, NCV)

Now we turn to a prayer perspective and gesture that has gone seriously out of fashion in its personal intimacy and its cosmology. Today we're most often taught to think of God as the ground of being, or the Oneness of all things. Spiritual writers emphasize not the separateness of ourselves from God, but the togetherness of us and the divine—and they explain how looking outside ourselves is to misunderstand where God is and how God functions. Looking "up" for God is a worldview to overcome—we're not supposed to see God up there anymore. All of this is wise teaching, and a helpful corrective.

Still. Everyone who has spent time in art galleries and museums is familiar with the old trope. The "Old Masters" (European, pre-1800) often showed biblical figures and saints with eyes and hands raised upward. I think, for instance, of paintings of Moses by Giovanni Francesco Barbieri in which Moses looks exactly as one might expect him to appear at a moment such as this:

> Now all of Mount Sinai was wrapped in smoke, because the LORD had descended upon it in fire; the smoke went up like the smoke of a kiln, while the whole mountain shook violently. As the blast of the trumpet grew louder and louder, Moses would speak and God would answer him in thunder. (Exodus 19:18-19, NRSV)

Or the hundreds of paintings of Saint Francis you encounter in museums around the world. Some of them have him with hands in his pockets, almost as if he needed to keep them there to avoid floating into the sky.

So why return to this old-fashioned practice—of looking up with fear, wonder, and anticipation when expecting to receive what God wants? Francis did, but that's not the only reason, or the real reason, I'm suggesting we try it now.

There are ways of experiencing God that are in our bones. In our genetic makeup even. For many of us, what's described of Saint Francis in these accounts is a gesture that still makes prayerful and powerful (even if not theological) sense. Like the author of Exodus, the psalmists (see Psalms 121 and 123 in addition to Psalm 19 already quoted above), the Hebrew prophets (Second Isaiah), and Jesus teaching the Lord's Prayer, Francis knew God in the gesture of turning his eyes and hands toward the heavens. Call it "the sky," if you have to, but don't avoid it only because it doesn't make sense.

There are so many things I do that make less sense than this.

"Skydaddy," I've heard as a perjorative for people like me who still sometimes talk to my "Heavenly Father." Comedian George Carlin had a famous routine mocking those who turn to an "invisible man who lives in the sky." Well, Francis would throw his arms up, and search with his eyes up too, for divine guidance. God was not only inside of him. God was "out there," and this gesture was Francis proclaiming: all of my yearning is for You.

I don't think he ever stopped to consider the rationale. Contemporary French philosopher Helene Cixous has said, "*Knowing* is not *believing*. Knowing does not believe. Knowing is without fever and without life.... One must not believe in miracles. If you believe in miracles, then there are none."[12]

So Francis stands alone "in the wood in contemplation," as the texts tell us, and not only that, but "with his face lifted up to heaven." Being alone is important—solitude is essential for wellbeing—but aloneness without the other elements of this way of praying would mean nothing at all. In a later scene, near his death, Bonaventure says that Francis' face was raised "as usual" to the heavens, and then the theologian explains why: "his attention directed entirely toward that glory, he began to praise the Most High because, released from all things, he was now free to go to him." I think of my children, before they could walk, pointing toward the thing that they were also crying about, unable to reach it. It's like that.

On other occasions, when he is in the woods by himself seeking God's guidance, or simply praising the Creator, he's doing so with his face turned upwards and also "his arms extended towards God." Let's not make this something that it wasn't. Francis knew that God wasn't in the sky any more than God was actually in the soil or in the birds and fishes. This was a gesture of the embodiment of his very creatureliness, humility, and most urgent desire.

—

Find the story: LF 19, BML 7.3
Consider a scripture: "Raise your eyes on high and see who has created these stars, the One who brings out their multitude by number, he calls them all by name; because of the greatness of his might and the strength of his power, not one of them is missing." (Isaiah 40:26, NASB, modified)

And "Let my prayer be set forth in thy sight as the incense: and let the lifting up of my hands be an evening sacrifice." (Psalm 141:2, BCP)

6 Standing between those who fight

Visiting Siena with Brother Masseo, Francis discovers that two groups of men are involved in a pitched battle. They are out to kill each other. It sounds like gang activity to those of us brought up on *West Side Story* and *The Godfather*. The text actually says their fighting already involves knives, and two men are now dead, which makes it seem like a scene out of the novel Pope Francis used to recommend, *The Betrothed*, by the Italian writer Alessandro Manzoni. Feuds and revenge were common in medieval towns and communes.

Now, this is a moment in the textual tradition when we have to be careful—because at such times it usually says that Francis began preaching. Preaching.

When you see a reference to Francis or one of his contemporary fellow friars "preaching" you shouldn't imagine a priest in a pulpit or behind an ambo, but something more like a minstrel and storyteller. Francis went to the fields to "preach" to people tending olive trees. He walked along the shore to "preach" with fishermen. The earliest Franciscans privileged time spent with the poor and with lepers. There was a universality to the language and purpose of Francis' preaching that might sound superstitious if it wasn't instead reflective of a generous understanding of where God is and how God works.

In fact, Francis and his brothers were often viewed in opposition to the clergy who ran churches, because it was so often that the Franciscans were "preaching" not in church buildings, and not in the ordinary ways. For this reason, clergy sometimes looked at Francis as the competition. And this wasn't helped by the friars' emphasis on bringing a "new word" to the people with their preaching. After all, was something wrong with the "old word" they heard from the priest at mass? Francis advised his fellow friars: "May you announce and preach God's praise to everyone in such a way that praise and thanks may always be given to the All-Powerful by all people throughout the world at every hour and whenever bells are rung."[13]

He also famously said, "Let all the brothers pray—by their deeds." In other words—words are not what was most necessary. Very often they were preaching penance—the need to turn one's life around, to go in a new direction—not with words (and definitely not with use of a pulpit) but with examples of folly, and singing using love song tunes turned to more pious purposes. There was also this advice: "Let the brothers preach in every way,"[14] meaning there are many ways to communicate God's presence, truth, and will.

In this particular instance of Francis' preaching, when he got in the middle of the two groups who were fighting with fists and knives, the text says: "He got between them and preached with such passion and holiness that they were all convinced to make peace." I don't see a preacher in that scene so much as I see a man with a reputation for no longer partying with his friends begging some guys he probably knew all too well to pause, breathe, shake hands, and go home. Consider another way.

Francis had a way of walking toward, rather than away from, trouble. "If the highest aim of a captain were to preserve his ship, he would keep it in port forever," theologian Thomas Aquinas once said. Francis could relate to that. Preservation of things-as-they-are never seemed to cross his mind. Francis had things to get done, and facing conflict head-on was sometimes simply unavoidable.

There was no pretense of "preaching" when Francis spent a couple of days walking to Gubbio, directly north of Assisi, either. The people there sent for him, asking for help with a wolf problem. This wild animal was killing some of their citizens, making it so that children couldn't play outside, and people couldn't walk safely alone. When Francis arrived and heard their stories, the first thing he did was go out to meet the wolf. Standing between the wildness and uncertainty of that beautiful creature and the concerns of the people of the town, Francis brokered an agreement. Gubbio would feed its hungry non-human sibling for the rest of its life and the wolf would never again menace its human siblings. It worked. People in Gubbio to this day remember the Wolf of Gubbio as a reformed, converted, sacred animal. Artists imagine him most often with a halo circling his furry head.

Another time in Assisi, years later, church and government officials were at odds with one another. The bishop and the mayor, both Catholics (big surprise), were fighting. The bishop excommunicated the mayor and the mayor issued a proclamation saying that no one in the city may sell or buy anything to or from the bishop. They'd grown to despise each other and made this plain to everyone. When Francis was sent news of it, he was already lying in bed with the disease that would end up killing him, so he couldn't visit them in person. He instead wrote a stanza of his now-famous "Canticle of the Creatures" and asked his brothers to sing it to the bishop and the mayor. First, he asked them to come and be together at the same place at the same time. He wrote:

> Blessed are those who live in peace,
> for You, Most High, will crown them.

Francis knew what the Buddhist teacher Thich Nhat Hanh would later often express so beautifully—that we have to begin to see all of the reasons why we become angry, why we feel angry. "We cannot speak about anger, and how to handle our anger, without paying attention to all the things we consume," he taught, "because anger is not separate from these things."[15] Thay, who was always so practical in his advice, pointed to the food we eat, the company we keep, and everything that we consume through our senses. Are they leading us to be gentle, or to be something else?

Francis' "preaching" was always about encouraging a Christian witness that is "a conversion to mercy and to a humble pardoning love."[16] Those two angry Catholics—the bishop and the mayor mentioned earlier—melted as the friars sang sweetly the words Francis had composed for them. Then they asked each other for forgiveness in front of everyone in town. Those who were there, who saw it happen, called it a miracle. This is the kind of ordinary miracle that filled the scenes of Francis' life. It's replicable.

—

Find the story: LF 4, AC 84
Consider a scripture: One of my other favorite, more recent saints is Therese of Lisieux. She used to say: "When you are angry with someone, the way to find peace is to pray for that person and ask God to reward him or her for making you suffer." That's a practice that actually works; I suggest you try it.

And the Jewish mystic and founder of Hasidism, the Baal Shem Tov, once said: "Once [we] are aware that everything is God—one of the fundamental secrets is—there is no more separation."[17] Ponder that the next time you're at odds with someone.

7 Becoming tender

It is immediately upon returning to Assisi, having failed as both a crusader and a knight, that Francis for the first time seems to have a profound experience of God. Chronologically, this experience comes at the head of the line, before all the others in this book. And it comes to him as what we call "grace"—divine gift that is totally unexpected, certainly unearned—in ways that surprise the young man, not to mention all of his former friends.

Unable even to move, or, the text says, to speak, we learn that "He was suddenly filled with tenderness."

Standing nearby were all of his old friends—hangers-on mostly—who valued the frivolous and shallow Francis they'd known as teenagers, the now enigmatic guy who had once paid for things and was fun at a party. They couldn't conceive what was happening because, unlike their friend, they hadn't yet met God in order to know themselves.* They saw Francis undergo this sensitivity to the divine and it made no sense to them at all. "What are you thinking about—a woman?" they ribbed him. To which Francis naively or dreamily responded,

*In a homily, Oscar Romero once said, "People do not know themselves unless they have encountered God. That is why there are so many me-worshipers, so many arrogant people, so many self-centered worshipers of false gods."

not really knowing where it all was headed, "Yes. I was thinking of a woman more beautiful than any of us has ever seen."

His angry father becomes even angrier at the insult of his son turning tender, when what he wanted him to be was tough, strong, and worldly powerful. So Francis' father gathers a posse to search for the young man, to straighten him out, and when Francis hears of it (most likely his mother warns him), he goes into hiding for a full month. Even when he emerges from hiding, and makes his way on the streets of Assisi once again, his old friends and previous neighbors "threw mud and stones at him." No one wanted to allow a transformation of gentleness and tenderness to take place in the guy they used to like so much.

Soon, other strange changes take place. Francis begins to walk more slowly, careful of what he steps upon. How to walk reverently over rocks, he ends up teaching his friends to do. Then, I imagine they leave him altogether and finally. How crazy he must have seemed then! People prefer the familiar, and when someone close to them changes so completely they cannot help but feel it as criticism. Was something wrong with how we used to be together?

Then come the stories of Francis talking with birds, and freeing rabbits and fish from capture. These accounts also are filled with references to his "tenderness," and also "sweetness," not simply as something felt as an emotion, or spoke to others (because he didn't talk about it), but as a way that he was becoming in the world around him.

The accounts of what happened then, which were written by less-than-sensitive people, even say that "the irrational creatures recognized his feeling of tenderness toward them." This was a breakthrough that was incomprehensible to others, and an encounter of God that, although he couldn't yet grasp it, Francis was willing to experience, and let it lead him. What a fool he was.

Power and influence, even simple life and liberty, were created by nothing to do with tenderness. Francis' was the era when knights carrying banners of the cross marched across Europe and used their weaponry to dominate and subdue Jews, Muslims, infidels, Christians of the wrong sort. Men raped women simply as plunder, and beheaded their enemies rather than discuss differences. There was little to no understanding of strength in peace, let alone tenderness. Power and domination were how things were done. These were the ways of men.

Even the pope, at that time, was not so much a spiritual leader as a political and military one, with armies of his own. And across the Silk Road from Europe was Genghis Khan, Francis' exact contemporary, conquering China and Central Asia with similar forms of brutality. His Mongol armies killed millions of people. He too was known as "great." When Francis went to see the Sultan in 1219, Genghis Khan was not far away, just across the Euphrates in the midst of conquering Baghdad. Any sort of tenderness among leaders in churches or anywhere else was countercultural.

This is perhaps why the Franciscan movement grew dramatically—because people sensed there was something different about it, and about Francis. His first biographer sums up the Francis effect like this:

> He proclaimed the word of repentance to all and announced the word of God in simple words, but with a great heart. At the outset of all his addresses, he proclaimed peace and pre-fixed all of his letters with a salutation using the word of peace. On account of these things, many people who had previously hated both peace and salvation [meaning,

> "church"], with the Lord's cooperation, came to embrace peace with all their heart.[18]

Have the ways and means of power really changed much over the centuries? I don't think so. Only the technology to implement and exert that power has improved. This is why the letter that Thich Nhat Hanh wrote to U.S. President George Bush in August 2006 is so simple, poignant, and frankly, Franciscan. The U.S. war in Iraq was ongoing at the time. And Thay told the President about a dream he had the night before and how upon waking, "I thought of the situation in the Middle East; and for the first time, I was able to cry."

> I cried for a long time, and I felt much better after about one hour. Then I went to the kitchen and made some tea.

What a fool. Without a doubt, whoever in the White House read that letter, thought this.

But how very relevant its teaching was, and is. Thay said that day: "Mr. President, I think that if you could allow yourself to cry like I did this morning, you would also feel much better. It is our brothers that we kill over there. They are our brothers. God tells us so, and we also know it.... [W]ith some awakening, we can see things in a different way, and this will allow us to respond differently to the situation."[19] We need awakenings of tenderness.

—

Find the story: TC 6-7, 10, 21, 58-60
Consider a scripture: "When Jesus saw the crowds, he went up the mountain, and after he sat down, his disciples came to

him. And he began to speak and taught them, saying: 'Blessed are the poor in spirit, for theirs is the kingdom of heaven. Blessed are those who mourn, for they will be comforted. Blessed are the meek, for they will inherit the earth. Blessed are those who hunger and thirst for righteousness, for they will be filled. Blessed are the merciful, for they will receive mercy. Blessed are the pure in heart, for they will see God. Blessed are the peacemakers, for they will be called children of God.'" (Matthew 5:1-9, NRSV)

It isn't easy. "Gentleness, self-sacrifice, and generosity" work together in a life, Mahatma Gandhi used to say.

8 Saying no to yourself

Most of Francis' spiritual practices and experiences of God were divine gifts, and by this I mean he did nothing but walk into them. This one is a bit different. Here, Francis ratcheted willpower, overcame slothful moments, fulfilled his duty, and generally put his soul to better purposes. "One isn't lazy about what one loves," writes Aldous Huxley in one of his novels (*Eyeless in Gaza*), and that's what the theme of saying no to yourself is about.

To start with the most obvious example, Francis came from money but gave it away at age twenty-five. This happened in two waves. First, he said no to some of the privileges afforded the son of a wealthy merchant from a good home—selling all his fancy things, and leaving behind his horse. But then he had lots of money in his pockets, and that made him uncomfortable, so when he came upon a priest in a very poor old church, he gave it to him. To put this in a broader context, capitalism began in thirteenth-century Europe and Francis was one of its enemies.[20]

Francis wanted no more special treatment, but unsure of how to make that happen, given his father's attitude toward money, work, and power, Francis ultimately had to run away from home. Still, they lived in a tight-knit community; there was no hiding for very long. His dad dragged him back and locked Francis in the basement. Not long after that, he said no to both money and a monied future—and said "no" definitively to his father—by removing the fancy clothes he was still wearing when his dad confronted him in public before the bishop of Assisi, accusing him of disobedience. With the whole town watching, Thomas of Celano's account has the bishop saying, as an aside (to us—not to Francis, or the people watching him that day), "Only the flesh, like a wall, was separating him from a vision of God."

From this time on, Francis said no to his desires in large and small matters. With a feeling of happiness that he was continually asked to explain, he showed that he didn't want to indulge in things that the poor could not join in too, such as fine food, first class travel (meaning, by horse, or with security), or even secure housing. This is part of why he chose not to become a monk: there was no safer place to live, then, than behind the thick stone walls of a monastery.

He also said no to his fear of getting sick. He'd been terrified of people with leprosy, moving to the other side of the road if someone afflicted came near. It was a somewhat irrational fear, and probably driven by a repulsion he felt in front of ugly and deformed things, learned from his culture, his family, and church.

This changed one day when he passed by yet another sick man. Francis rode quickly on, disgusted as usual, but then something happened. Suddenly, Francis brought his beast to a stop in the road, and began to rebuke himself. A spirit of compassion and generosity had been poking its head up through the soil of Francis' heart for some time, and now was when he would listen, act, and allow it to come to full flower. The young man leaped from his horse and ran back to the spot where the leprous man stood, without word, watching the scene like a bystander. Francis embraced him. If there was anyone there to see it, they must have been gobsmacked.

Then, as can happen in a life, one gesture of change led to another and another. There's a holy spirit in all this, but there is also that bit of determination and will. Francis wasn't thrown from his horse in the direction of the sick man—but he was perhaps pushed gently that way.

Several years later, when it came time to write a few words of spiritual "Testament" (an autobiographical writing of his), Francis began the first paragraph by saying that everything began when God "gave" him the "ability to do penance" by leading him among lepers. He finishes that paragraph saying, "shortly afterward, I got up and left the world." *World* meant the same thing "the flesh" had meant in those words of the bishop of Assisi a few years earlier: all that he'd learned that was wrong—again, from culture, family, and church.

Most essential is the happiness Francis realized through this form of renunciation: saying no to himself. Changing course. Learning the freedom that comes, not from infinite choices, but by becoming and doing who we are and what we're called toward. For all people, this cannot happen without also learning to say no. As Richard Rohr has said, "All great spirituality is about letting go."

As he matured and became more experienced in this spiritual practice, Francis understood himself as a small part in an enormous and complicated world. He accepted the mystery of himself and of those around him. He looked with gentle eyes, seeing more, and demanding less. As Czeslaw Milosz says in one of his beautiful poems, "Love means to learn to look at yourself / The way one looks at distant things / For you are only one thing among many."

I think this expression of faith is being rediscovered by people today. We know we're not in control; our religions told us that we once were, but now we know better than that. And it *is* better. Techniques for "saying no" to ourselves have existed in religions since time began, but they often look wrong in practice and have names such as "mortification," which just sounds wrong. The essential point is much simpler: there's a freedom that comes from divesting, unloading, and detaching.

I love how Zen teacher Julie Seido Nelson expresses this as learned from her practice of sitting meditation:

> Some degree of discomfort...is inevitable, especially on long retreats. Learning to sit still, even when you've got an annoying itch or an aching knee, is a crucially important practice. Our brain tells us that we have to
>
> SCRATCH!
>
> MOVE!
>
> DO IT RIGHT NOW!
>
> Not paying so much attention to the demands of our brain is the beginning of insight. We start to understand how much our brain lies to us. We start to learn to be okay with reality as it is, even when painful, instead of always trying to fix it right away. As we continue to practice, we come to find that our entire perceived self and world are delusory. (This doesn't mean we aren't individuals, or we don't fight injustice. But realizing that we have habitually filtered everything through a screen of 'what's in it for me?' progressively frees us from attachment to our perceptions and beliefs.) It all starts with not scratching an itch.[21]

—

Find the story: TC 8-10, 13-15; FW 250
Consider a scripture: "The goods of God, which are beyond all measure, can only be contained in an empty and solitary heart." (St. John of the Cross) "[P]ut off your old self, which belongs to your former manner of life and is corrupt through deceitful desires.... [B]e renewed in the spirit of your minds and...put on the new self, created after the likeness of God in true righteousness and holiness." (Ephesians 4:22-24, ESV)

Compare this to "The cause of suffering is craving. The cessation of suffering comes with the cessation of craving." (The Buddha's Four Noble Truths, 2-3)

9 Remembering your hermitage

Metaphors used by Zen and Catholic monks to describe concentration have included a cat with a mouse, a hen sitting on her eggs, and a fish swimming in a lake that is never caught. The monks had techniques for staying focused on their prayers and meditation which they talked about with each other and then taught to novices who came to join them.

I like the cat and mouse one best. It's basically this: be like an old cat with a mouse in your meditation or prayer practice—hold it lightly, be relaxed, but also never let it get away. Your mind and disposition should be casual, the way a cat looks like it might allow the mouse to wander off—though it never quite allows that to happen. Meditate and pray with this sort of curiosity and playfulness. It's only the kitten, not the mature cat, who out of too much anxiety and nervousness overhandles the mouse, allowing the little thing to pass.

The fish metaphor is wonderful too. St. Romuald, in his Rule for Camaldolese hermits (ca. 1000 CE, in Tuscany), said: "Sit in your cell as in paradise. Put the whole world behind you and forget it. Watch your thoughts like a good fisherman watching for fish.... The path you must follow is in the Psalms—never leave it." Every fisherman knows that time spent on the river or in the lake is about more than pulling a live one from the water.

Beyond the metaphors, there were also concrete practices to aid monastic spirituality. Fasting, for instance, was supposed to concentrate the mind. Or eating food that others would find disgusting, so as to remove any use of sustenance as pleasure. Lack of sleep, too, was believed to have a concentrating effect. (I can't help but think how that last one is precisely the opposite!)

Francis of Assisi may have learned some of these techniques and tricks. But he also had no real monastic mentors. Shocking—given his status as a Roman Catholic saint par excellence—is the fact that Francis tells us in his own words, "No one else showed me what I was supposed to do." He deliberately didn't become a monk, and he seemingly found his own way to his ways of spirituality.

Imitating Jesus in the gospels is what Francis set out to do, feeling that this is the life God wanted from him. Even when it rubbed up against the expectations of religious leaders; Richard Rohr is spot-on when he says: "It's why he trained his followers to be ministers for the gospel instead of seeing them as ministers for the church."[22] There was some anti-intellectualism in this on Francis' part. He thought very little of a scholarly approach to faith, and never partook of it. He wouldn't have known, for instance, but would've approved of St. Ephrem the Syrian's fourth-century words: "Blessed is the one who has not tasted the bitterness of the wisdom of the Greeks. Blessed is the one who has not relinquished the simplicity of the apostles."[23]

When Francis traveled to a new place, he practiced what he referred to as "praying the Lord in the heart"—while walking, while talking, and being in the presence of fellow travelers. Where he learned this, we don't know. (Ephrem the Syrian wrote about the same practice and monastic students ever since have learned it from him and others like him.) Francis puts it beautifully:

> For wherever we are and walk, we may always
> have our hermitage with us,

"because Brother Body is our hermitage, and our soul is the hermit who remains within his hermitage to pray to God and remain fixed on him." What is a "hermitage," after all, but the place where a solitary kind of monk lives all alone.

Francis was no monk, and he certainly wasn't a solitary one—a hermit—so why would he use the metaphor of a hermitage to talk about prayer? The answer is simple: he's talking metaphorically, as Jesus was when he used similar language. Your hermitage is the place that Jesus told his disciples to find, and go to, for prayer, rather than praying "like the hypocrites" who "love to stand and pray in the synagogues [and churches] and at the street corners, so that they may be seen by others." Jesus says, instead: "Go into your room and shut the door and pray to your Father who is in secret, and your Father who sees in secret will reward you." What room is he talking about?

Not the extra bedroom in your house—first-century homes in Roman-controlled Palestine had no such thing! This wasn't the American suburbs. Imagine a family of fourteen living in two rooms, without indoor plumbing. What Jesus refers to as "your room," or in other translations, "your closet," Meister Eckhart calls "the ground of your soul." The same metaphor is used in the book of Revelation when it has God saying, "Listen! I am standing at the door, knocking; if you hear my voice and open the door, I will come in and eat with you, and you with me" (Rev. 3:20, NRSV). It is the place you go to be with God Alone. It is in fact probably the *only* place where you can meet God that way.

In other words, the remember your hermitage way of experiencing God might just as well be "Remember your soul." And go there.

—

Find the story: FW 251, MP 37
Consider a scripture: "Here's what I want you to do: Find a quiet, secluded place so you won't be tempted to role-play before God. Just be there as simply and honestly as you can manage. The focus will shift from you to God, and you will begin to sense his grace." (Matthew 6:6, The Message)

There is much in the Bhagavad Gita to compare this to, on the subject of action and inaction. Perhaps start here: "For the person desiring to attain yoga, action is said to be the mean. For the person who has already attained yoga, quiet [or tranquility] is said to be the means." (6:3)

10 Asking for help

Yes, Saint Francis wrote, "No one else showed me what I was supposed to do." He didn't have a mentor or a guru, and didn't submit himself to one of the routine systems of tutelage and authority in the Catholic Church.

That doesn't mean he was a cowboy. Leaders everywhere and since time began have behaved as if leadership means never showing weakness. Never asking questions. Never changing your mind. Francis initiated and then led the fastest growing spiritual movement Europe had ever seen, yet he was frequently questioning himself, his motives, and where he was headed. He showed plenty of weakness. And often changed his mind.

Just imagine. He was even questioning himself several years after the Franciscan movement (they didn't call it that then) had started: *Should I have gotten married?*

Also early on, when they were gaining hundreds of new adherents a month, Francis asked himself: *Am I supposed to spend my time in contemplation and prayer, as service to God, or should I be active in the world helping others?* He enjoyed both. He loved praying alone in those caves—where he'd remember his hermitage, and feel close to God and God's embrace—and he was one of many religious people who challenged the idea, made famous by a monk named Anselm of Canterbury a century earlier that contemplation was only to be found and nurtured in a cloister. But Francis also loved hands-on caring for people in need; it felt good to be doing what Jesus told him (everyone) to do—feeding and clothing people in need.

In each of these experiences Francis would become quickly and thoroughly immersed. So to which should he devote himself? He was a "both feet in" sort of person. He needed to find the correct direction.

He also knew better than to assume he could easily discern God's will all on his own. So he asked two people he trusted—Clare of Assisi, the first female Franciscan, a family friend, and one of the first to follow him into religious life; and a man named Sebastian, another one of the first friars. Clare and Sebastian both promised to think and pray about Francis' question and get back to him with what they heard as an answer.

Sylvester was the first priest to join the movement, and it's perhaps important to point out that he and Francis had a checkered history; Sylvester wasn't always Francis' biggest fan. In the early days, when Francis and Brother Bernard (the very first follower) were distributing money to the poor, it was Sylvester, a parish priest, who approached Francis on the street in Assisi and said: "You never paid me for the stones I gave you!" Francis had begged stones from Sylvester and used them to repair falling down churches. So Francis thrust his hand into Bernard's pocket and grabbed a handful of money, quickly handing it to Sylvester. Sylvester palmed it, turned on his heels, and went home.

Soon thereafter Sylvester felt guilty for his demand, and about that exchange with the earnest convert. He probably didn't need the money. He had demanded it with a sense of righteousness. And since that time, Sylvester observed the young man's sincerity, genuine piety, and how he was making positive changes in people's lives. So much so that Sylvester was convinced to come and join the friar movement himself. Which means there must have been a scene that we don't see in the texts when Sylvester also was on the street giving away all of his stuff, as Bernard had done.

By the time of our story, Sylvester has become one of Francis' most trusted guides, and a friend. (Bonaventure would also remember Sylvester, decades later, as a great contemplative and mystic of the earliest Franciscan spirit. This aside is a reminder that we all can change, over time.)

Well, Sylvester comes back to Francis first, with a message he's received saying that God sees what Francis has done in his life to cultivate "a harvest of souls" and it is very good. This means Francis simply can't run off to the mountains and live as a contemplative. He is supposed to be feet-on-the-ground working for the kingdom of God.

Then Clare comes to Francis and basically confirms the same. In today's parlance we call what happened here, "spiritual direction," in that the wisdom, experience, and compassion of another human being can act as a window through which we see meaning for our lives. The spiritual writer Henri Nouwen explains, "Seeking spiritual direction, for me, means to ask the big questions, the fundamental questions, the universal ones in the context of supportive community."[24]

The great sixteenth-century Spanish Carmelite mystic, Teresa of Avila, expressed her relationship with her spiritual director in ways that further illumine Francis' experience with Sylvester and Clare: "I saw that, out of his own experience, he understood me. And that was all I needed; for I did not understand myself then as I do now, and I could not describe what I was experiencing."[25]

When Francis heard the word from the two of them, the tradition says he kneeled while listening—as if they were holy words he was receiving—and as soon as he heard what they had to tell him he responded with, "All right, let's go!" and jumped to his feet.

—

Find the story: LF 13, LT 30
Consider a scripture: "Get wisdom; get insight: do not forget nor turn away from the words of my mouth. Do not forsake her, and she will keep you; love her, and she will guard you." (Proverbs 4:5-6, NRSV)

And Henri Nouwen, in his book *Spiritual Direction*: "A spiritual life doesn't necessarily lead to tranquility, to peace, or to a beautiful feeling about ourselves or about how nice it is to be together with others. The chipping-away process can hurt. It might mean being lonely in a place where you never wanted to go. It might lead you to a vocation you never sought. It might ask you to do uncomfortable things. Or it might ask you to obediently and routinely do comfortable things that are not very dramatic when you prefer adventure. The spiritual truth is that God is at work in each of us and in our communities and families. Often, the companionship of trusted friends allows us to see how God is at work."[26]

11 Making a cross with your arms

We see Francis doing this in anticipation of receiving the will of God for his life.

Stand upright and hold your arms out straight from your sides. What does this symbolize? What does it feel like? This is the cross of Jesus on Calvary, where he did as his Father instructed. The shape of it is sometimes called "cruciform," which as either an adjective or a noun literally means shaped like a cross. But that doesn't mean cruciform imagery and symbolism began at the time of Christ. The Egyptian symbol *ankh* was cruciform long before the time of Jesus. And the Romans were crucifying people before Christ. In fact, they invented the word "excruciating" from the same root that comes "crucifixion," to mean—well, you know.

There are also cruciform melodies in music, and there is cruciform DNA, which is, I'm sure, a lot older than two millennia. Most importantly, cruciform arms at one's side predates Christ by millennia. This is a much more ancient form of devotion.

We have found cruciform figurines and cave drawings that go back to the Stone Age and no one seems to know for certain the meaning of those arms shooting out from human sides. Our best guess is that, long before the Romans invented the horrible form of capital punishment, there was some understanding of such a death leading to an equally astonishing new life. Joseph

Campbell, the expert in comparative mythology from a generation ago, speaks to this:

> What has always been basic to resurrection, or Easter, is crucifixion. If you want to resurrect, you must have crucifixion. Too many interpretations of the Crucifixion have failed to emphasize that. They emphasize the calamity of the event. And if you emphasize calamity, then you look for someone to blame. That is why people have blamed the Jews for it. But it is not a calamity if it leads to new life. Through the Crucifixion we are unshelled, we are able to be born to resurrection. That is not a calamity. We must look freshly at this so that its symbolism can be sensed.[27]

Human beings knew resurrection long before they knew crucifixion.

In the Middle Ages, the arms began to raise a bit higher from the waist. There was a Latin word, *orans*, meaning "pleading prayer" and relates to the lifting up hands in an attitude of questioning and supplication. Francis would have known this, and he would have known the verse in the New Testament book of 1 Timothy believed to be written by the Apostle Paul that says, everywhere people pray they should be "lifting up holy hands without anger or argument" (1 Timothy 2:8, NRSV). Medieval Christians learned this from the Hebrew psalmists, for example—"Hear my prayer for mercy when I call to you for help, when I lift my hands toward your most holy place" (Psalm 28:2, Book of Common Prayer).

In making this gesture, Francis is seeking direction—but he only knows this form of openness because he learned it from his Lord. In his life, Francis was also intentionally and deliberately cruciform, meaning, in his life he aimed to give as Christ gave, in love and humility for others.

As for all the rest, the origins of this spiritual practice can look to us a bit...superstitious. But medieval Christians understood that coincidences and serendipities were signs, never inconsequential, and that life was often lived in liminal places between the real and unreal that are often indiscernible from one another, or from God. They looked less intently than we do for reasons for everything.

This is what the sources tell us about Francis' love for the cross. His love was such that he taught his friends to see crosses *everywhere.*

> In whatever place a church had been built, even when they were not near it, but could glimpse it from a distance, [the friars] would turn toward it. Prostrate on the ground, bowing inwardly and outwardly, they would adore the Almighty saying, "We adore you, O Christ, in all your churches . . ." just as their holy father [Francis] taught them. What is just as striking is that wherever they saw a cross or the sign of a cross, whether on the ground, on a wall, in the trees or roadside hedges they did the same thing.

Did you catch that? They would be walking along the road, or through town, and glimpse the shape of a cross in the formation of earth on the ground, in the design of something on a wall, in the way that branches were grown together or torn apart in the trees, and in how hedges were kept. Their eyes were trained to see crosses, and when they saw them, they prostrated themselves and prayed, "We adore you, O Christ." This was a simple, powerful, inexplicable experience of God that they found solid.

Francis saw also a cross when birds flew as flocks in the air. This happened perhaps for the first time at that moment when Francis preached to the birds, in what has become one of his iconic scenes. His friend, Brother Masseo, recorded the event and remembered what Francis said, alone, to a flock of birds along the roadside. "The air is all yours! Your Creator loves you! Therefore, be grateful always and praise him," he said to creatures who he thought of as sisters. And when he was done talking, his sisters stretched their wings, Masseo remembered, as Francis made the sign of the cross before them. Then Masseo's account implies that the birds took to the sky and flew away in a cruciform shape.

Anyone who has watched geese overhead, honking and flying in this formation can picture the scene easily. I'll bet Francis was looking up, feeling the inspiration that people in every place and time have felt at such a sight. As naturalist Lyanda Haupt writes in *Mozart's Starling*, "*Inspire* is from the Latin meaning 'to be breathed upon; to be breathed *into*.' Just as I ponder the migration of birds, I ponder the migrations of inspiration's light breeze. If it's not with me, where is it?"[28]

I also imagine if Francis were around today he'd be fascinated by the cruciform shape that our DNA undergoes in repair mutations or in musical compositions known as the Bach Motif. He'd probably look at the forms of cruciform design used for strength and stability in engineered structures.

In practical terms, Francis would kneel or stand in prayer, arms out at his sides, palms up, as in a gesture of both giving and receiving. This is the experience of God on recommendation here. You will try this, I hope, whoever you are. Make a cross with your arms, when you pray, as if the cruciform form and shape is not accidental. Do this in openness and receptivity, in hope of divine grace and surprise. Without asking why.

—

Find the story: TC 45, LF 13
Consider a scripture: Always, Francis was learning his practice from what he read about Jesus. "They brought to [Jesus] a deaf man who had an impediment in his speech; and they begged him to lay his hand on him. He took him aside in private, away from the crowd, and put his fingers into his ears, and he spat and touched his tongue. Then looking up to heaven, he sighed and said to him, 'Ephphatha,' that is, 'Be opened.' And immediately his ears were opened, his tongue was released, and he spoke plainly." (Mark 7:32-35, NRSV)

Consider how this symbolism is similar to, and different from, the lotus symbolism of ancient Indian prayers such as: "My soul, listen to me! Love thy Lord as the lotus loves water; buffeted by waves its affection does not falter. Creatures that have their being in water, taken out of water, die."

12 Crying "Who are you, God?! And who am I?"

This is the anecdote about Saint Francis that makes him, more than any other religious figure, the one who speaks to my heart. Even when people begin calling him a living saint, Francis has doubts. Even when his closest followers believe he is the source of all that is good in the Catholic Church, he remains unsure of who God even is. Gestures with his hands—inquiring, pleading, questioning beyond himself—take on more meaning with the words here.

At such times, when this happens, we watch Francis doubt his vocation. One time it was, *Should I have gotten married and raised a family?* He apparently still had terrible thoughts, and secret sins. Other times it was, after eating too much, or committing a private sin, wondering to himself and others: *Am I a fraud?*

This way of experiencing God returns us again to example #2 (Praying alone in the woods), which was then extended in #5 (Lifting hands and eyes to the sky), and is now extended yet again. It turns out that this is a sequence of three—Francis would often go to the woods to pray all alone. He would raise his eyes and arms toward the heavens. And now, we see that these are some of the words he would pray: "Who are you, God? And who am I?"

We have a specific scene, upon Mount La Verna, where Francis has gone for forty days of fasting and prayer. Note his need for solitude. "Why is solitude so potentially powerful for all kinds of people?" a team of researchers recently asked, before concluding: "Think of it as the ultimate place to do what you want (autonomy) and be who you are (authenticity)."[29] This is strikingly true for Francis of Assisi, and again why we relate to him easily: his desire for solitude, in order to figure out who he was and what he was supposed to do next, in contrast to a pious Catholic understanding of a saint, that there are no longer existential questions to be asked and answered.

He's taken a friend with him, Brother Leo, but asked Leo to only check in on him once per day. On this occasion, Leo comes up the mountain in the early hours of the morning while it is still dark and the moon is high in the sky. It is Sister Moon that provides Leo the light needed to see where he is going on the path, and then to see Francis kneeling in the near-distance—"his face raised toward heaven and his arms extended to God."

Leo hears Francis' voice and his prayer. "Who are you, God?! And who am I?" Francis keeps repeating this doubting prayer "and nothing else," the text tells us. It is a yearning, as were all those times when he was looking and reaching up, but it was also a repeated ritual. Somehow, the meaning of a religious life is found in the repetition of certain simple, eternal questions.

The crying out loud is essential to what's happening, to what Francis is doing.

This is not quiet. And neither is it passive. It is also not entirely private. I like how the theologian George Pattison, in a dense, reflective book called *A Philosophy of Prayer*, talks of how prayer can sometimes be distinguished clearly from what might otherwise simply be described as "trying to think clearly about one's situation." He uses an idea from the Jewish philosopher Franz Rosenzweig called "vocativity," when someone speaks certain words "to" or "as if" to "someone." And then, it is not simply that the words are addressed to someone—or, Someone—but this vocativity is, more pleadingly or defiantly perhaps "crying out for a self-understanding that the self cannot give itself."[30] Yes, that's it with Francis!

I also like what Ramana Maharshi said: "The question, 'who am I?' is not really meant to get an answer, the question 'who am I?' is meant to dissolve the questioner."[31] Again, yes!

Or maybe it's even more than all of that. It may be that such eternal, elementary, reaching prayers are not so much a human *expression* of need and desire, as they are a desire for God that comes from that human place inside us where God resides. Because then, "Who are you, God? And who am I?" would be like a connective tissue of spirit to Spirit, or even more, of one unified spirit speaking as if in a single voice. In this way, one of the early Hasidic rabbis, Pinchas of Koretz (eighteenth-century Ukraine), taught that sometimes "The prayers you pray are the very presence of God."

—

Find the story: DF 9.37
Consider a scripture: "Ask, and it will be given you; search, and you will find; knock, and the door will be opened for you. For everyone who asks receives, and everyone who searches finds, and for everyone who knocks, the door will be opened." Also, "The kingdom of God is in the midst of you." (Matthew 7:7-8 and Luke 17:21, NRSV and RSV)

And the Zen master-monk, Dizang—that's his Japanese name; he's a bodhisattva by other names in other schools of East Asian Buddhism—said, "Not knowing is most intimate."[32]

13 Sitting on the ground

We can't just leave "not knowing" there, because Francis was all about not knowing many centuries before it became a thing to talk about. For him, not knowing took a deliberate and practical form that resembles what we saw in Roshi Bernie Glassman and the Zen Peacemakers movement he founded in 1994. They were committed to paying little attention to intellectual matters for the sake of living with a naïve openness in their communities. They summarized this in three clear principles:

> *Not Knowing*: letting go of fixed ideas about yourself, others, and the universe.
> *Bearing Witness*: to the joy and suffering of the world.
> *Taking Action*: that arises from Not-Knowing and Bearing Witness.[33]

Sitting on the ground was when Francis was by himself, in the midst of a life devoted to not knowing, bearing witness, and taking action. He was on the ground to identify with what's there, and to refuel. Like raising his arms to the sky, sitting on the ground was an embodied expression of his faith. To sit on the ground, like a creature. To be low to the ground as one who is lowly, humble, and poor—like, for instance, the migrant Mary and the infant unwanted Christ in the manger, in Bethlehem.

It was also a bit crazy. Who did such things?! Throughout history, what others perceive as madness has always been the catalyst for new ideas, breaking superstitions, and hearing anew the voice of divinity.[34]

One day at Greccio, Francis was staying with his brothers there when they were also expecting one of their religious leaders to arrive for dinner. The table was festively set and a menu prepared. The narrator tells us: "It happened that the brothers of that place on Christmas day itself prepared the table elaborately because of a visiting minister, covering it with lovely white tablecloths which they obtained for the occasion, and vessels of glass for drinking."

One imagines Francis refusing to sit at the table, taking a place on the floor instead.

In fact, when he arrives to eat the meal, and sees the table set so finely, Francis quietly leaves and dons "the hat of a poor man," it says, and carries a staff down to the road, where he begins to beg for his bread as a friar is supposed to do. A little while later he knocks on the door, like a pilgrim might do, and shows the friars who answer it what he has to eat. He was, of course, making a point. Taking on flesh, in such poor circumstances, the holy Child from his first hour had nothing, was identified with the poorest of the poor.

There are other, more literal examples of Francis sitting on the ground—as when he stepped down from leadership in his religious order. At the next general-chapter meeting, with thousands of friars in attendance, there we see Francis the founder sitting at the feet of the new minister-general occasionally asking for permission to speak.

His humility was not put on for show, but arose from his understanding that all creation prays. We see this in the "Canticle of the Creatures," the first vernacular Italian poem ever written—the one that praises Sister Moon and Stars and

Brother Wind. And Francis' poetry was prophetic in the way suggested by Czeslaw Milosz: "The poetic act both anticipates the future and speeds its coming."[35]

Equally cinematic was the time when Francis was asked to preach to his human sisters—the women gathered with Saint Clare at San Damiano convent—and instead of preaching in the way we think of it today, Francis sat on the ground quietly before them. He poured ashes around himself in a circle. Then he got some more ashes and poured them on his head. For obvious reasons we call this the "Ashes Sermon." After some minutes of silence, Francis stood and began to recite Psalm 51, a prayer of confession:

> Have mercy on me, O God, according to your loving-kindness;
> in your great compassion blot out my offenses.
> Wash me through and through from my wickedness and cleanse me from my sin.
> Create in me a clean heart, O God, and renew a right spirit within me.
> (Book of Common Prayer)

There are similar stories in other traditions. For example, from the late eighth-century Zen master Yaoshan Weiyan: "He walked to the large chair at the front of the hall where he would sit when giving Dharma talks, and then, without saying a word, turned around and went straight to his room. Later, his attendant asked him, 'Why didn't you speak?' and Yaoshan replied, 'There's no need to say anything.' Then he added, 'If you want to study intellectually, you can go to a philosopher. I don't need to speak. I just practice with you.'"[36] Saint Francis knew nothing about Zen or Yaoshan, but he likewise was practice-led, and for him not knowing related directly to sitting on the ground without fuss. Or instead of fuss. From that humble place, he wasn't asking any questions; he was just experiencing God.

—

Find the story: AC 74, TS 207
Consider a scripture: "[I]f a person with gold rings and in fine clothes comes into your assembly, and if a poor person in dirty clothes also comes in, and if you take notice of the one wearing the fine clothes and say, 'Have a seat here, please,' while to the one who is poor you say, 'Stand there,' or, 'Sit at my feet,' have you not made distinctions among yourselves, and become judges with evil thoughts?" (James 2:2-4, NRSV)

And this, "All Things Pray," an interpretive reflection on the *Yotzeir Or* portion of the Shabbat morning service in synagogue: "It is not you alone, or we, or those others who pray; all things pray, all things pour forth their souls. The heavens pray, the earth prays, every creature and every living thing prays. In all life, there is longing. Creation is itself but a longing, a kind of prayer to the Almighty. What are the clouds, the rising and setting of the sun, the soft radiance of the moon, and gentleness of the night? What are the flashes of the human mind and the storms of the human heart? They are all prayers, the outpouring of the boundless longing for God."[37]

14 Talking with non-human creatures

Francis is of course the saint who preached to birds. Isn't that what everyone, even those who couldn't care less about saints, know of him? (Far fewer remember an incident that came soon thereafter which we call "The Stilling of the Swallows.")

It happened for the first time in the Valley of Spoleto as he was walking alone, probably discouraged because very few of his fellow human-animals showed interest in his preaching. It was then when he noticed a lot of birds gathered along the roadside in tree branches. I find it interesting, first, that he noticed this at all. His biographer says that he took notice because "they didn't fly away, as they usually do."

Next, the text tells us three of the bird species. They were not to Francis—or his earliest chroniclers—simply *birds*. They were doves, crows, and magpies. This was like knowing their names. The Wisconsin poet Jacob Riyeff refers to knowing the names of species (plants, in his case) as like "Adaming creation beyond the Fall."[38] That says it very well. On that road, the friar was hearing soft and comfortable coo-OO-oo-oo'ing of doves combined with the harsh insistence of caw-caw-caw and raspy squawking.

It also says that as Francis rushed to meet the winged strangers, he greeted them "in his usual way." This means: "May the Lord give you peace"—a greeting that became a trademark for Francis, and shows how he regarded these creatures as similar to his human siblings. The story of this preaching to the birds then concludes with the statement that "From that day on, he carefully exhorted all birds, all animals, all reptiles, and also insensible creatures, to praise and love the Creator."

In contrast, we know how we arrived at the place where we find ourselves now—separated from creation, literally and figuratively "walled off" from most of what else breathes in the universe. It's simple really: our ancestors latched onto that one line from the Hebrew scriptures that has God telling the first humans to behave as if they were meant to rule the earth and "subdue it" (Genesis 1:28), rather than love it and live within and among it. And our forefathers and foremothers decided to disregard the corrective to this that Francis of Assisi offered 800 years ago when he reminded us of our fundamental connection with other creatures, non-human animals, birds, fish, insects, even invertebrates. This was before industrialization, the discovery of fossil fuels, internal combustion engines, and air travel. Now it seems there is no turning back.

There's a gospel story Francis knew that we no longer do. Francis knew it as every child in medieval Christian Europe did; a story from Jesus' boyhood that was part of the lore of the Savior's earthly life. It doesn't come from Matthew, Mark, Luke, or John but from an apocryphal gospel written a century later. It's about the five-year-old boy Jesus pondering the lives of birds. After a heavy rain, young Jesus is playing near a stream with water and clay and begins to fashion sparrows from clay between his fingers. One by one he makes twelve sparrows until someone points out that it is the Sabbath, not a day to be making—or building, or creating—anything. Then they point this out to Jesus' father, Joseph, who comes over to scold the boy. Jesus' response is to clap his hands and say to his handmade creations, "Go. Take flight," and the clay figures turn into very real sparrows and fly away.[39]

About 150 years ago, it began to be common to disbelieve in God's existence. I wouldn't want to begin to trace how and why this happened. But one example of this is how it became common to associate a feeling of kinship with nature with disbelief. Thus, a great nineteenth-century English novelist could paint one of his most interesting skeptical characters (Angel, in Thomas Hardy's *Tess of the D'Urbervilles*), passing from religious belief to atheism, saying that then:

> He made close acquaintance with phenomena which he had before known but darkly—the seasons in their moods, morning and evening, night and noon, winds in their different tempers, trees, waters and mists, shades and silences, and the voices of inanimate things.*

The "natural" was made to contrast with the "supernatural," as if they were in opposition. As if Francis had never been alive talking with birds, calling the moon his sister, and handling stones with care.

This is the same man who cared for bees in wintertime, setting out honey and wine for them. For whom one of his first dramatic acts—and his life was full of dramatic acts—was purchasing a pair of doves in the marketplace only to then toss them into the air, setting them free. Francis would even ask his brothers, if they absolutely had to cut down a tree, not to cut it whole, but to simply remove branches so that the trunk may continue to thrive.

He would go out into the road and lift earthworms from the pavement after a rain, placing them back in the grass. He held crickets in his hands, thanking them for singing as they

* From part 3 of the novel, "The Rally," chapter 20.

were made to sing, knowing that it must be praises to God their creator. He even asked his fellow friars to consider walking reverently over rocks. Who did such things, then (or now)? There was no seminary or monastery, then (or now) that taught a person to care for worms, consider the birds as siblings, and walk reverently on the natural ground. With rare exceptions, mystics speak of experiencing God in *themselves*, not in other creatures. I wish we could say these teachings of Francis' have greatly impacted the church and Christian practice, but they really haven't yet.

One of his significant inheritors is Henry David Thoreau, who was neither secular nor saint, but he saw, touched, and heard the divine throughout the natural world. Thoreau referred to nature as "a newer testament, the Gospel according to this moment"—a sentiment I suspect Francis would appreciate.[40] And, like the saint who cared for worms and bees, Thoreau once defended his love for walking in swamps by saying that they were his "holy of holies."

Most of all, I hope you will look differently at the usually quaint story of Francis preaching to the birds. As we've seen in prior chapters, "preaching" never meant what we think it means now. And those doves, crows, and magpies along the road were not objects of the young man's attention, but subjects of his shared life. It was as if Francis was putting his arm around them, talking with them in conversation. Such relationships—with creatures not like us—were openings to the experience of God.

—

Find the story: TC 58-59, 23; LF 13

Consider a scripture: "See, the former things have come to pass, and new things I now declare; before they spring forth,

I tell you of them. Sing to the LORD a new song, his praise from the end of the earth! Let the sea roar and all that fills it, the coastlands and their inhabitants." (Isaiah 42:9-10, NRSV)

And consider how the Jesuit priest and scientist Pierre Teilhard de Chardin came to understand certain holy sacraments: "Since once again, Lord—though this time not in the forests of the Aisne but in the steppes of Asia—I have neither bread, nor wine, nor altar, I will raise myself beyond these symbols, up to the pure majesty of the real itself; I, your priest, will make the whole earth my altar and on it will offer you all the labors and sufferings of the world.... Into my chalice I shall pour all the sap which is to be pressed out this day from the earth's fruits..."[41]

15 Praying at night

This experience relates to a few of the others we've looked at, but also stands alone as a tried-and-true way of experiencing God in any religious tradition.

In Jewish scriptures, Jacob wrestled with the angel during the night, and Daniel got up in the wee hours to pray alone and in secret. Early Christian monks did as the Rule of Benedict advised them, rising "in the middle of the night" to pray. Monks still do this, wherever a contemplative religious order exists. "Vigils" is what the pre-dawn prayer service is called, from a Latin word meaning "to watch." Watch for what?

The Qur'an speaks lovingly of those who sleep less at night and who ask for forgiveness in the pre-dawn hours when prayer isn't obligatory (see 51:17-18). Islamic poet Hafiz held prayer vigils at night in fourteenth-century Persia and wrote many of his best poems in those moments. "All through the night is peace," he expressed in ghazal 246.

Was Francis alone praying at night? This was a period of time when most of those around him apparently did not do this. For example, the first source referenced below has it that Francis, "after Compline, laid down to sleep so that he could then get up to pray in the middle of the night, as he often did while the others slept." Why did he do it? Francis doesn't explain, but it probably had to do with his desire to be alone with God—and not wanting to show off.

There's an ancient Christian tradition that 3 a.m. is the ideal time to pray. Some say this is because physical temptation is greatest in the dead of night. Others suggest that since this is when the world is quietest, prayers are clearest to hear. Still others—and I suspect Francis was one of these—believe that too few people hold up Saint Paul's injunction to pray "constantly" at the really inconvenient times.

On this particular occasion, a young novice follows Francis outside, in secret, and sees the saint in conversation not only with Christ, but the Blessed Virgin, St. John the Baptist, St. John the Evangelist, and various angels. Sometimes the stories of what took place around Francis at these times, of what friars thought they saw from a distance, were bizarre.

There was also the night Francis spent alone in prayer in the garden of an Assisi church when a chariot of fire appeared above him, and above the chariot was a brilliant ball of fire. Perhaps the observers who were noting these details were drowsy or hallucinating; the essential point really is that remarkable things happen between us and God when done in quiet and in secret. In every instance of his praying at night, the practice of keeping vigil—wakefully watching—is taking place. There are committed people still doing this today. "Keeping vigil" is the act of staying awake during a time when others are asleep, attending to someone who is sick or dying, or as a means of protest, or finally, to just pray.

Shemira, in Judaism, is one example of this. The Hebrew means "watching" or "guarding" and the practice refers to the custom of at least one person at a time watching over the body of someone who has died, constantly, from the time of death until the moment of burial. A loved one is not to be left alone—certainly not to the cold chemicals and procedures of a funeral home.

Francis lived with the sense of never wanting God to be left alone or ignored. He never lived in a traditional monastery, and he certainly was never what is called a "choir monk," whose responsibility is to always be there to pray the liturgical hours. But as people of all religious traditions or none have known for millennia, silence is more than the absence of sound. Silence is a hearing posture. Writer George Prochnik gets at this when defining silence as "the particular equilibrium of sound and quiet that catalyzes our powers of perception."[42] There's an openness that takes place in us when we are surrounded by an absence of noise and echo that is not so much an absence of something, but a presence of something. And this is not just a clever way of suggesting the presence of God. I mean, for example, we often become present to ourselves in a way that would otherwise not have been possible.

And what is it, then, that we're tuning to, that's present in us? When Francis was praying aloud at night in the garden in Assisi—everyone seems to have understood that the chariot and ball of fire that were seen were indications that the saint was being illumined with divine light and heat. There were other such moments in Francis' life—one thinks of the mystical stigmata, for instance, of which it is best to say nothing at all. The saint never spoke of it; nor should we try to understand it. And perhaps that's the point. Zen teacher Shunryu Suzuki wrote in his classic *Zen Mind, Beginner's Mind*, "It is a kind of mystery that for people who have no experience of enlightenment, enlightenment is something wonderful. But if they attain it, it is nothing. But yet it is not nothing."[43]

These moments are examples of a mystic's experience of ecstasy—a mystic's word, from the Greek *ekstasis*, meaning "standing outside oneself." To do that is much more about humility, for Francis at least, than it is about its opposite: wanting to stand apart.

—

Find the story: LF 27, TC 47-8, BO 4.4

Consider a scripture: "Evening, and morning, and at noon, will I pray, and cry aloud: and he shall hear my voice." (Psalm 55:17, KJV)

And from the book of Daniel: "Then was the secret revealed unto Daniel in a night vision. Then Daniel blessed the God of heaven. Daniel answered and said, Blessed be the name of God for ever and ever: for wisdom and might are his: And he changeth the times and the seasons: he removeth kings, and setteth up kings: he giveth wisdom unto the wise, and knowledge to them that know understanding." (Daniel 2:19-21, KJV)

16 Making soup for today

Take no thought for tomorrow, Jesus taught, as if to extend a Shabbat practice to every day of the week. This one is almost universally ignored today. Ask the most intense Jesus follower you can find if they make plans for tomorrow and they'll say of course I do. This is one of those teachings that we grownups are supposed to understand as exaggerated language, not a literal instruction.

Francis didn't know from exaggerated language, not when it came to the sayings of Jesus recorded in the New Testament Gospels.

Even in the early sources, when this example is spoken of, it is in remembrance, past tense only, saying "many friars observed this practice in many places for a long time." And where this anecdote was first recorded there is an opening paragraph that frames the account in the context of idealism. It says, "Blessed Francis was of such purity that, from the beginning, when God told him that he and his brothers should live according to the holy Gospel, Francis desired and set out to observe it to the very letter." In other words, even the early friars who lived with him, and watched him every day, had trouble believing it.

Then comes the soup—this way that Francis experienced the presence of God in the preparing of soup. The very first example given of Francis living for today is given that he instructed the friar whose job it was to prepare the soup never to soak the beans overnight. This doesn't mean that the friars did not eat soup with beans; I think it simply means that they were satisfied to eat soup with beans that were perhaps still a bit crunchy. The cook-friar who listened to Francis' instructions would begin soaking beans only when the liturgical prayer hour of matins was concluded, meaning first thing in the morning.

A first impulse, hearing this, is to dismiss it as pie-in-the-sky idealism. Try living a grownup life in North America today (or almost anywhere else), for instance, without at some point renting an apartment, or buying a home—which Francis wouldn't do. There was even a time when he visited the friars in an Italian town who were building a home for themselves, contrary to the Franciscan Rule, and Francis immediately scampered onto the roof and began ripping shingles from it.

Try living a grownup life today without using a credit card or putting money in a bank account. Francis would not. There was no means-to-an-end thinking in his makeup. For example, the Dominicans, who emerged at the same time as the Franciscans in the early thirteenth century, shared some of Francis' commitments to poverty and simplicity, but they also took a realistic and pragmatic view that theological studies were like "bending the bow" of an arrow—a necessary act to fulfill their commitments to evangelism and preaching. Francis wouldn't make those compromises. Eat soup with crunchy beans, and preaching without theological subtlety is just fine.

He tried to live by an alternative economy. One early biographer seems to have really "caught" this, going out of his way then to use economic terms for describing changes in Francis' life: "He removed himself from the chaos of business and made himself a salesperson of the gospel" and "He went seeking better pearls, until he came upon one particularly precious one."

We've surely gone too far in the other direction. In response to pie-in-the-sky accusations when looking at Francis' idealism, we usually regard planning for tomorrow as something that every responsible person is obliged to do. But for a moment consider how separating from the dominant money culture of the world might be good for you—even if only in small measures.

Civil rights activist and scholar Rabbi Abraham Joshua Heschel wrote a book in 1951 that quickly became a classic. It's called *The Sabbath* and points to how the Jewish concept of a day of rest is meant to pull human beings outside of that world money culture for a mere twenty-five hours a week. It is easy to see why politicians, always wanting to measure success by economic growth, might stand against this, but it's just as easy to see why ordinary people desperately need it. Heschel writes, "Man is not a beast of burden, and the Sabbath is not for the purpose of enhancing the efficiency of his work." In other words, don't interpret Sabbath as simply rest-time. He also wrote: "The solution of mankind's most vexing problem will not be found in renouncing technical civilization, but in attaining some degree of independence of it."[44]

If that sounds like idealism, consider how there's an element of *carpe diem* in this teaching too. Bob Dylan says, "When you ain't got nothin', you got nothin' to lose." The book of Ecclesiastes says: "For the living know that they are to die, but the dead no longer know anything. There is no further recompense for them, because all memory of them is lost. For them, love and hatred and rivalry have long since perished. Never again will they have part in anything that is done under the sun. Go, eat your bread with joy and drink your wine with a merry heart, because it is now that God favors your works." (9:5-7, NAB) Jews read this every year during the season of *Sukkot*, when they construct temporary huts with roofs of branches and leaves designed so that the sky is visible through them ("modeled after clouds...clouds of glory," says the Talmud), reminding them that this life is temporary, and life itself is precious. Francis and his friends knew God in this way.

Seize today—by thinking only of it. The happiest people are those who learn to live in the present, such that they don't think about the past and future. As a result, they don't spend much energy in the directions of fear and hope. I think of the happiness of a dog, for whom "I love you now; please love me too" is the meaning of life. Francis and his friends managed to live this way while still having the minds and understanding of human beings.

They also did not beg more alms than they needed for a single day. They didn't build permanent homes, but relied on temporary dwellings. I'm sure it wasn't easy—you couldn't find domestic quiet in a Franciscan lifestyle in that first generation, just as the disciples of Jesus did not have it—but there were other benefits.

I'm not saying this is what everyone is called to do. I don't often follow this myself, but Francis clearly experienced God in this way of living and I wonder if the distance many of us feel from the divine today is in proportion to how well we've set-up our planning for tomorrow.

—

Find the story: AC 52, JS 3
Consider a scripture: "In you, O Lord, I seek refuge; do not let me ever be put to shame; in your righteousness deliver me. Incline your ear to me; rescue me speedily. Be a rock of refuge for me, a strong fortress to save me. You are indeed my rock and my fortress; for your name's sake lead me and guide me; take me out of the net that is hidden for me, for you are my refuge. Into your hand I commit my spirit; you have redeemed me, O Lord, faithful God. You hate those who pay regard to worthless idols, but I trust in the Lord." (Psalm 31:1-6, NRSV)

17 Deepening desire

The biblical prophet Daniel became a touchstone for early Franciscans. If you look at texts in the Hebrew scriptures about him (the books named for Ezekiel and Daniel) you'll see someone who paid close attention to dreams and dreaming, and who paused in solitude and prayer several times a day. Shia Muslims share this view of Daniel as a prophet too, even though Daniel doesn't appear in the Qur'an. In Franciscan spirituality, he was remembered as a "man of desires," and as such, looked upon as one of the models for a Christian wanting to develop contemplative habits.[45]

Desire. Is it a longing, a yearning, a craving, a wish? These aren't usually regarded as good things—something to cultivate. In Judaism, for instance, the Hebrew phrase *yetzer hara* in Genesis chapter six says that God looked on all humankind—"the thoughts of their hearts"—as evil (Genesis 6:5, NRSV). Those thoughts in people's hearts sound like desires or cravings, suggesting that they can be dangerous or not good for you. God destroyed the world with a flood after looking on humankind that way, seeing those tendencies.

In other contexts, desire is again understood negatively. Craving and wishing leads to grief and fear, says an ancient Buddhist teaching. A Buddhist does not cultivate desire, because desire is the cause of suffering. Instead, a Buddhist aims to curb desire, to control all that feeds into the building of desire, in order to achieve equanimity.

Francis shows some agreement with this when he explains that a primary reason not to possess wealth is because then you'll worry about losing it, and you'll worry to the point where you'll feel you might have to be violent toward someone who comes to take it from you. It's better to simply not have it in the first place.

The French literary critic Rene Girard speaks of desire as little more than imitation: we want only what we see others wanting. This helps to explain the envy, rivalry, and idolatry that fills human hearts—and that God was disgusted with, in the Noah era of Genesis 6. Francis' use of desire was not to do with these things, because he renounced envy and idolatry and the like. Francis insisted on being like, and equal with, everyone else. That was his desire, which he cultivated.

Francis sometimes experienced God through a stoic-like response to hardship and difficulty—as in the example in this book about practicing joy in small hardships (see #4). But most often, for Francis, passivity and quietude were not the measure of a person alive with God; a stirring heart and conscience was. His faith is about passion and desire, and as such, imitative of Christ.

Francis' desire showed in his body. It was as if he couldn't contain in himself the faith that was building from growing desire. So we see Francis running toward the leper, stripping off his clothes, singing sacred songs in the moonlight, walking across a desert to see the Sultan. Holding his arms up in the air and crying out with a loud voice in the middle of the night. A stoic doesn't do those things.

Francis' contemporary, the beguine Hadewijch of Antwerp taught the virtue of "noble unfaith." The problem with faith for most people, according to the Dutch mystic, was how it dampened desire by answering every question and creating contentment. Faith is yearning, she said, not its opposite. Theologian

Holly Hillgardner summarizes this, in Hadewijch, beautifully when she says that noble unfaith is about never "letting desire by satisfied."[46]

Desire is much more than emotion. Desire is not how you feel so much as it is what takes hold of you. And its beginning in us is basic and visceral. My friend Ronald Rolheiser says that what is most basic in all of us—such as sexuality and creativity—is where desire begins. Ron writes, "Human desire is a complex thing. There's a surface and there's a depth, and in every one of our longings and motivations we can ask ourselves this: What am I really looking for here? I know what I want on the surface, here and now, but what am I ultimately longing for in this?"[47]

Francis' desire was what is often called "affective yearning" in Christian mystical literature, and in his life this was expressed in every which way. Even and especially if you are alone, Francis would say, do your praying, or say your prayers, while standing. Bonaventure tells us that even when he was chronically ill, Francis would "stand upright," never leaning. If on a journey and a canonical "hour" for prayer was upon him, he would stop, stand upright and attentive (see #20). Even in the rain, Francis would do this: standing in the elements, but seemingly unaffected by any discomfort, focused entirely with reverence and devotion on what he called "receiving that food which is God himself."

The "desires of the flesh" were to be avoided. By this, Francis meant impulses that prompt people to sin, and ways that "the world" gets its claws into you that are no-good, leading to greed, selfishness, impatience, haughtiness, roughness. Steering completely clear of what might harm you. But the word "desire"—and more importantly, the passion it stands for—was something Francis sought to deepen. Like iron attracted to a magnet. This meant, for him, love with the soul for what the soul knows and loves best. And he expressed this with his hands and feet and heart.

A generation after Francis, Bonaventure, who was the minister-general of the Franciscans, looked to Francis' stigmata experience upon Mount La Verna as the epitome of a contemplative's deepening desire. Summarizing this, Bonaventure wrote: "For we enkindle desires within us in two ways: by an outcry of prayer which makes us wail from anguish of heart, and by a lightning-bolt of insight which turns our mind most sharply and ever watchfully to flashes of light." It's a poetry that Francis couldn't have mustered himself to describe his feelings, but it catches just right how cultivating the holy flame of desire is a way to know God most intimately.

—

Find the story: BO 10.6, MP 22
Consider a scripture: "Take delight in the LORD, and he will give you the desires of your heart." (Psalm 37:4, NRSV)

And, sometimes Hadewijch wrote passionate poems in which "love" meant both the human and the divine:

"O love, were I love
And with love to love you, love
O love, for love grant that love
May know love wholly as love."

18 Resigning positions of leadership

I never promised that each of Francis' ways to God would be worldly wise or commodifiable, only that they would be replicable. This one will certainly never become an app on your phone.

After spending many months in and to and from the Levant and the Nile Delta, where Francis visited the Sultan Malik al-Kamil at the height of the Crusades, hoping for friendship and peace, he returned to Umbria and the Papal States to find what? His spiritual movement had changed. Friars had started to "move on" from Francis' principles, and began to turn the Friars Minor into something looking and acting more like a traditional monastic or religious order. Ties with Rome and its cardinals and curia were tightened, buildings were built, and many friars were becoming priests.

Their founder had taught that following Jesus meant taking seriously Sermon on the Mount teachings like "Don't store up treasures on earth, where moths and vermin destroy, and where thieves break in and steal," and "Don't think about tomorrow" (Matthew 6:19, 34). So he forbade his smart, young, earnest brothers from pursuing advanced degrees (expected of clergy), and constructing buildings such as churches, where friars do good things, and houses, where friars might like to know they'll have a place to sleep for more than a night.

Francis resigned his leadership, seeing that his vision was

no longer what they wanted. He installed a new vicar as the spiritual guide for the friars. From this point on, for the remaining five years of his life, there would be a sadness as well as a desire to see the brothers return to the original principles.

On one occasion, the cardinal who now had a very close relationship with the new Franciscan leadership, wanted to raise up some of the friars to more positions of leadership throughout the Church. Francis begged him not to. "My brothers are called Minors, and they shouldn't want to become greater." Francis went on to plead with the cardinal—who would later become the Bishop of Rome, Pope Gregory IX—not to raise up any Franciscan brothers to leadership positions. They are supposed "to live in the footprints of Christ's humility," Francis told him. It then says, in the texts, that Francis was reminding everyone of what the original Rule of their religious order had said, that they were to, most of all, care for lepers and live in leper houses alongside the sick. How different this was from what the new leadership was aiming for.

They have been "called lesser, so that they will not want to become greater," Francis said to the cardinal that day, as it was remembered by another witness, and recorded in another text. "If you want them to bear fruit," Francis said, "keep them where they have been called to be, or bring them back to that station, if they are unwilling." It didn't work. When that lord was himself elevated to the papacy six months after Francis' death, the march toward Franciscan power in the Church continued quickly, despite their Rule. Within sixty years there were many bishops, archbishops, and then a cardinal (Bonaventure) in 1273, and the first of nineteen Franciscan popes (Nicholas IV) in 1288.

In contrast, consider the story of Brother Juniper. At a time when he'd already earned a reputation for saintliness and was known as one of Francis' good friends, soon after the saint's death, Juniper was asked to visit a nearby town to give a spiritual talk. He journeyed there by traveling down a long, straight road, such that he could see far ahead toward the horizon. There he glimpsed his hosts waiting for him with excitement and expectation. It almost looked like they had organized a party and a parade to welcome the great Brother Juniper!

But Juniper was one of the friars who took seriously Francis' original intentions about poverty, humility, and power. He looked far ahead and saw his hosts, but he also looked to the side of the road and saw children playing. He decided to stop and play.

The children were on a seesaw. There, Juniper stayed, playing with the children, bouncing up and down on the seesaw. This went on for a while until a few people from up the road began to wander down toward the playground. They saw Juniper there and bid him to join them. The people were waiting to hear his spiritual teaching! But Juniper didn't want to leave. He was having fun with the kids. Juniper was also puncturing a hole in the balloon of power that the people of that town were waiting to bestow upon him. He never approached that spot where they were greeting him with such fanfare. This was called "playing the fool."

The story of Brother Juniper is an extreme one, designed to make a point. Very few of us will follow that example today.

In fact, I'm not going to blow a lot of smoke and say that avoiding or resigning from positions of leadership is good for you. That you'll live longer, with less stress and more happiness, and all that. I'll simply say this: the humility that comes from not being in power is, according to Saint Francis, a decision that you can willingly make, and it is one of the ways to experience God—in this world and the next.

—

Find the story: MP 14; AC 49
Consider a scripture: "Blessed are the poor in spirit, for theirs is the kingdom of heaven. Blessed are those who mourn, for they will be comforted. Blessed are the meek, for they will inherit the earth. Blessed are those who hunger and thirst for righteousness, for they will be filled. Blessed are the merciful, for they will receive mercy. Blessed are the pure in heart, for they will see God." (Matthew 5:3-8, NRSV)

Compare to the "Great Spirit Prayer" of Chief Yellow Lark of the Lakota Sioux (late nineteenth century): "O Great Spirit, whose voice I hear in the winds and whose breath gives life to the world, hear me. I come before you, one of your many children, I am small and weak, I need your strength and wisdom. Let me walk in beauty and make my eyes ever behold the red and purple sunset. Make my hands respect the things you have made, my ears sharp to hear your voice. Make me wise, so that I may know the things you have taught my people, the lesson you have hidden in every leaf and rock. I seek strength not to be superior to my brothers, but to be able to fight my greatest enemy—myself. Make me ever ready to come to you with clean hands and straight eyes, so that when Life fades as a fading sunset, my spirit may come to you without shame."[48]

19 Kneeling before holy images

Experiences of God are not sought and found by following prescriptions or directions. They almost always come unexpectedly. That's where the word "grace" comes from.

Francis didn't have to have an experience of God when he kneeled in the abandoned church of San Damiano. It could have happened that he simply stopped, said a few words, and left. There was no one present to say anything about the divine to him, and the place was uncomfortable and falling apart. The walls were leaning and crumbling, a priest came and went occasionally, in duty, and rarely did anyone there see or care to pay attention to what was happening.

Francis was a young man who knew very little about religion. We get the sense that he "fell to his knees" in desperation, or simply hope, as people do, in nearly abandoned churches. He was also surely kneeling in veneration (the word means "bowing down") of what was there with him. Hanging above his head, to which the text says he turned his full attention, was an icon crucifix—which means a piece of painted wood showing the scene of the crucifixion of Christ upon it. After a period of time kneeling there—I'm guessing it was many days after his initial visit—Francis heard something in return for his prayers.

He may in fact have done more than kneel before the icon—Bonaventure says he prostrated himself. To prostrate means to lie flat on the floor. And as Francis prayed from that position he must have felt consoled. He cried, he heard God speak to him, and it seems that for a few moments Francis passed out. Makes perfect sense, in fact.

I love how the old text puts it, explaining what happened immediately next. It talks of how Francis felt inside: "He was shaken by unusual experiences and discovered that he was different from when he had entered." Then it continues without an apparent understanding that God has been heard many times before speaking with a voice in real time: "As soon as he had this feeling, there occurred something unheard of in previous ages: with the lips of the painting, the image of Christ crucified spoke to him."

This is the moment when Francis' conversion is said to have been perfected, or completed. When he came to his senses, he got up and began doing what he'd heard God ask him to do: repair that church in which he was kneeling.

You'll meet many people who have had religious experiences before divine images. Francis is not unique. It happens even today. I've known friends who kiss an image (an icon), or otherwise greet an image (a photo of one's guru at a home altar) like a loved one every morning. And I've known other people who relate to a particular image as if the image itself was a gift—a sort of "kiss" from God.

The Trappist monk and writer Thomas Merton was someone who felt spoken to by icons. When a Greek Orthodox friend gave him a hand-painted icon from Mount Athos of the Virgin Mary and Christ Child, Merton wrote the friend to say:

> I have never received such a precious and magnificent gift from anyone in my life. I have no words to express how deeply moved I was to come face to face with this sacred and beautiful presence granted to me.... I never tire of

> gazing at it. There is a spiritual presence and reality about it...which seems unaccountably to proceed from the Heart of the Virgin and Child as if they had One heart, and which goes out to the whole universe. It is unutterably splendid. And silent.... [This] icon of the Holy Mother came as a messenger at a precise moment when a message was needed, and her presence before me has been an incalculable aid in resolving a difficult problem.[49]

One couldn't experience such a holy presence without kneeling in one way or another. And one doesn't hear a word from God without such a posture.

The Sanskrit word *darshan* means "view" or "appearance," and indicates a holy practice in Hindu traditions of icons and images of gods. But more importantly, darshan means "to be seen," and the relationship is a reciprocal one. Those who see the divine are seen in return by the divine. That is how icons and icon crucifixes work in Christianity as well.

I'll give the final word back to the old text which again remained focused on how Francis felt—now, as he rose from the floor: "Francis was more than a little stunned, trembling, and stuttering like a man out of his senses. He prepared himself to obey and pulled himself together to carry out the command. He felt this mysterious change in himself, but he could not describe it."

Some experiences of God are not at all ordinary. They aren't supposed to be.

—

Find the story: BO 2, TS 10

Consider a scripture: "All these things my hand has made, and so all these things came to be, declares the LORD. But this is the one to whom I will look: he who is humble and contrite in spirit and trembles at my word." (Isaiah 66:2, ESV)

And in his eighth-century defense of venerating icons, St. John of Damascus said, "[Because a human body became God in Christ] therefore I reverence the rest of matter and hold in respect that through which my salvation came, because it is filled with divine energy and grace."[50]

20 Praying words of ancient texts

I mentioned this at the outset. For thirty years I've been keeping seed and suet feeders close by my living room windows throughout every season but summer. I've told myself how much the birds rely on me, and have taken comfort in the knowledge that I am helping them thrive. But the truth is that wild birds don't really need me. They are designed to live well on their own. In fact, human intrusions, some experts say, do more to harm wild birds than to aid them.

There's another reason I do it: I want to see them. I like seeing and hearing them talk. By bringing them into my domesticated orbit, I get to observe what is natural and wild up close—for my benefit, not theirs. Chloe Dalton expresses this beautifully on the final page of her memoir about a hare she cared for during the pandemic: "The sensation of wonder she ignited in me continues to burn, showing me that aspects of my life I thought were set in stone are in fact as malleable as wax, and may be shaped or reshaped. She did not change, I did. I have not tamed the hare, but in many ways the hare has stilled me."[51]

This is also surely, whether they realize it or not, why some Christians "pray the Hours," and why any religious person, despite their doubts and relying less on faith than their ancestors once did, still pray the words of ancient texts. To bring what's wild close to us.

As we've seen, Francis invented the friar as distinct from the monk. A friar is different from a monk in many ways, but not in this one. Francis prayed what's called "the Hours," meaning the Hebrew psalm readings—praises, blessings, laments—at regular times and intervals every day. These prayers were not his primary "work," or even in the top three, but they were still very important. This is a reason why he asked the bishop in Assisi, and then the abbot of the nearby monastery, for permission to regularly use the tiny chapel called Portiuncula, or St. Mary of the Angels, in the valley below the city. He wanted a place set apart for this kind of prayer.

By most accounts, Francis didn't mind praying religious texts even while traveling. We see him regularly stopping along the road, wherever he is, to stand and be silent, while praying set verses. This is a kind of devotion that makes less sense to people now than it once did.

Nothing happens in the world as a result of praying scriptures. The practice has no use in any measurable sense. In generations past, people prayed like this religiously, out of duty. It's just what you did. It's what you were taught to do. I still hear this rationale today, and occasionally I'll find someone who prays religiously in the way that Saint Francis once did: out of a sense of devotion that's not as much about faith and belief, as it is a kind of a priori understanding. Their devotion to God is essential, like eating every day, done largely without question or assertion.

One doesn't ask the moon why it comes out every night. One simply looks up and greets the moonlight.

This is why Francis, who was unschooled and struggled to read (his literacy was minimal), would reverence any piece of paper he found with writing upon it—because he thought that perhaps the writing might be from sacred texts. The only comparison in religion I can find for this attitude is not

Christian, but from the devotees of Krishna, who have for centuries believed that simply uttering his name is a many-faceted blessing.

And I think of the *gopis*, female cow herders, who in the tales of the tenth book of the *Bhagavata Purana* are drawn with love to Krishna. Krishna represents the divine and supernatural, and the gopis love him no matter how foolish, dismissive, and inattentive he may be toward them in the stories where he is a cowherd boy. Who, if they are devoted to the spiritual life, hasn't experienced these feelings when reflecting on their own God-relationship? My God is not often attentive to me either. But our devotion keeps ticking almost against our will, and this is expressed through the repetition of the words of our religious texts.

Francis didn't always feel so generous toward books and scriptures—as evidenced by his response to a young novice who was begging him for permission to obtain a breviary of his very own. To Francis, there was the ethical principle of not owning things, and that was his first response to the boy. Refer to your Rule: you don't need to own anything. But the novice persisted and much more important than simple poverty to Francis was his conviction that saying prayers doesn't make a person prayerful. He gestured pleadingly to the novice, pointing to his heart and head, saying, "I am the breviary!" That's how it ought to be anyway.

There was also the time when the mother of one of the friars came to ask for financial help. "We have nothing left in the house to give away," someone said. To which Francis replied, shocking everyone, "Give our mother the New Testament so she can sell it to care for her needs, for through it we are reminded to help the poor. I believe that God will be pleased more by the giving than by the reading."

Still. Francis would be walking the road, about the most

important business of reconciling people, bringing aid to the sick, and preaching his inspiring messages—but he'd still stop, pull out his breviary, stand there, and read aloud the texts for the day. It probably appeared ridiculous to some who watched him do this, but that wouldn't have mattered to him. Devotion was simply who he was.

Even a dedication to repeating words that he didn't necessarily understand was a way of being fully present and attentive, of connecting daily life and responsibility with divine energies that have been working for millennia. Daily exercise to keep him balanced and fit for everything else.

—

Find the story: MP 45, AC 104, TS 91
Consider a scripture: "Seven times a day I praise you" and "Pray without ceasing" (Psalm 119:164 and 1 Thessalonians 5:17, NRSV).

See also in the *Bhagavata Purana*: "God, this son of the gopi, is not attained as easily in this world by embodied beings, nor by the wise, nor by the knowers of the self, as he is by those who have devotion." (X,9,21)[52]

21 Making music, singing and dancing

As if drunk, Francis would sometimes sing love songs to God while walking alone in the woods, or while with others, and pretending with sticks to play a violin while crooning—which is an apt descriptor for what one early fourteenth-century text calls "tears," "groans," and "joy." He also loved lute-playing, even though religious people in his time associated this with vanity and sin.

He was, by his own description, a *jongleur*, which means "performer," but others call him a troubadour as well. This is not quite in keeping with the scholarly definition of the term: "The troubadours were poet-musicians composing in Occitan, the language of what is now the south of France."[53] However, those who listened to Francis sing his compositions—written in vernacular Italian, modeled after what he heard and appreciated from the Occitan—called him troubadour. They called him this even before his conversion, to describe the wooing of women Francis did in those days. When he fell in love with Poverty, instead, he turned that passion to religious uses.

Francis was consciously tapping into the playfulness of troubadour culture. We are "*jongleurs de Dieu*," he said, which means, we are "jugglers/clowns for God." A professional troubadour would sometimes employ a jongleur to travel with him, dancing and singing his songs, often wearing the most outrageous and colorful clothing. Their songs included protest lyrics, satirical tunes, laments (common during the Crusades, or even when medieval popes were so obviously caught in corruption), as well as burlesque. It was in fact a Franciscan who first said why should the Devil get all the best tunes.* But most popular of all were the love songs. These Francis knew well, and he composed his most famous one late in life, as a love hymn to Mother Earth and Creation itself.[54]

He was hymning for and to the Earth in the "Canticle of the Creatures," in which he located God and all that is sacred in this common home. There's no mention at all of heaven or the afterlife. Here are its first two verses:

> Praise to you, my God, with all your creatures,
> and especially our Brother Sun,
> who brings us the day and brings us the light.
> He is good and shines with splendor and glory.
> O God, he signifies you to us!
> Praise be you, Most High, for Sister Moon
> and all the stars.
> You're the one who set them there in the heavens,
> making them bright and luminous.

Such language was unheard of in Christianity at that time—and is rare even today. The "Canticle" is more like a divine revelation than it is example of a tradition. But it is possible to find similar praises and enthusiasm in other spiritual traditions. For example, one writer from the Nahua and Maya

*It should be noted that this emphasis on music was lost in later generations of Franciscans, especially when their spirituality was brought from Spain to New Spain (the Americas) in the sixteenth century, where the influence of Francisco de Osuna's *The Third Spiritual Alphabet* and its emphasis on the asceticism of avoiding pleasure, including music, had an impact.[54]

lineages, a native of Chiapas, Mexico, recently offered a song of Indigenous wisdom with these lines translated from Tzeltal: "Love the lunar wisdom! Love the solar joy!"[55]

Next in the "Canticle," Francis gets more specific, moving on to other vast, essential creations:

> Praised be you, my God, for our Brother Wind,
> and for air and clouds, calm breezes and all kinds of weather
> through which you uphold life in every respect.
> Praise God for our Sister Water,
>   who is so useful to us, and humble,
>   and precious, and clean.
> Praise God for our Brother Fire,
>   through whom you give us light in darkness.
>   Brother is bright and pleasant, mighty and strong.
> Praise God for our Mother Earth,
>   who sustains us and keeps us, and pops us grasses and
>   all of the fruits and flowers of various colors!

One of the many reasons why Nones, Dones, atheists, agnostics, and others sometimes steer toward him is that these verses of praise are not to a God on high, and they don't correlate salvation with the afterlife. They are instead in tune with the American poet Wallace Stevens when he versed: "It must be this rhapsody or none, / The rhapsody of things as they are" (from "The Man with the Blue Guitar").

—

Find the story: AC 38, 66; FW 246-48

Consider a scripture: "Much is said of what is spiritual, and of spirituality, in this, that, or the other—in objects, expressions.—For me, I see no object, no expression, no animal, no tree, no art, no book, but I see, from morning to night, and from night to morning, the spiritual.—Bodies are all spiritual.—All words are spiritual—nothing is more spiritual than words." (Walt Whitman, *An American Primer*, ca. 1860)

And this, from Henry David Thoreau's *Journal*: "God should come into our thoughts with no more parade than the zephyr [breeze] into our ears—only strangers approach him with ceremony. How rarely in our English tongue do we find expressed any affection for God. No sentiment is so rare as love of God." (March 11, 1842)

22 Forgetting what others think

The Q&A was over at a small university in the American Midwest where I was invited to give a talk on Francis of Assisi and early Franciscan spirituality. As people began to gather their things and leave, a small, older man made his way toward me at the front of the auditorium. "I'm in my eighties now," he said. I nodded, unsure where this was headed. "And I'm a retired priest."

I smiled broadly at him. "It is very good to meet you," I said. I love meeting clergy, and I'm honored whenever they do things like approach the younger non-ordained to ask a question after a talk. That's a simple humility often not found in the cloth.

Everyone else had wandered away except for me and the octogenarian. "I've read a few of your books on Saint Francis," he said.

"Thank you," I replied. "I hope you found something useful in them."

He nodded. But something clearly was still to come. Then he leaned in, as if to tell me a secret. He said: "This past summer, I became friends with a frog in my pond. I'd like to know, in all seriousness ... do you think that's crazy?"

Big smile from me. "Absolutely not," I said. In fact, in the late nineties and aughts I lived in a log cabin in West Hartford, Vermont where a late neighbor, a poor hermit named Joe

Ranger, was known to have communicated daily with a beaver named Billy in the pond across from his cabin. Stories of him were part of the oral legend of that place.

When I shared the Q&A anecdote a few days later with an Eastern Orthodox friend he replied with a story of his own. He said, "Some thirty years ago at a women's monastery in Romania, the nuns were going out of their minds during divine services on a warm day. The windows of the church were open. The frogs in the pond beside the church were making such a racket that the nuns couldn't even pay attention to the service. Finally, the oldest nun strode outside in a snit. When she strode back into the church a minute later, there was complete silence outside. The nuns standing near her asked, 'What did you do?' 'I told them to shut up!' the older nun said. There was never again any noise from the pond. The community assumed that somehow the elder nun had gotten the frogs to leave. But when the pond was drained for maintenance some months later, there sat all the frogs at the bottom, still not making a peep."

Then I told a Jewish friend about my eighty-year-old priest friend who is friends with frogs, and he reminded me of an old Hasidic story. "Remember the rabbi who went down to the pond every morning to pray with the frogs? 'It takes a very long time to learn their prayer,' he told his students."

There's no story about Saint Francis and the Frog. But there are plenty of occasions when Francis did things that would be puzzling, even scandalous, in the eyes of others—and he didn't care. He didn't worry about what others would think. If he had, he wouldn't have experienced God so completely in the craziest of ways.

The occasion when he visited the Sultan in Egypt near Damietta is perhaps the most prominent example of this. Over the centuries, the Church has spun it to make Francis the hero who went to vanquish a Muslim foe for Christ, but that doesn't seem to be what happened. Francis and some companions took a very long journey from lands comfortably controlled by the Pope in Rome to visit with the man who was in charge of combatants facing papal troops on crusade to the Holy Land. There is no indication that Francis considered what others would think of his crossing enemy lines to sit and talk with the enemy.

The Church tried its best to make this occasion into an evangelistic event, but that's not what it was. They even made it into a martyr's crusade, as if Francis were seeking to die a martyr's death at the hand of the scary "Saracen"—that's the term they used during the Middle Ages to refer to any and every Arab, Turk, or follower of Islam. (No one knows for sure where the word originated, and why, but it seems that it stems from an Arabic noun, *sariq*, which means "thief.") Saracens were the ones—lumped ingloriously altogether—who the Christians thought had stolen the Holy Land from them. "Saracens and other unbelievers," is how you often find people who were the object of Christian disgust in the crusading era quickly categorized and dismissed. I'm sorry to say that the account in *The Little Flowers of Saint Francis*, written about a century after the event took place by someone who wasn't there, describes the people with whom Francis met that day as "cruel men" who never allowed "a Christian to pass through without being killed." They sought to make it an extraordinary saintly miracle event.*

The Christians were in fact the militant ones in this scenario. Francis wanted only to meet the man who seemed to frighten everyone else. Why does it have to be this way? It didn't, Francis believed. He wanted to meet the Sultan as a

*Worse than the account in *The Little Flowers* is the contemporaneous reportage of Jacques de Vitry, the bishop of Acre when Francis visited the Sultan, calling Malik al-Kamil a "cruel beast" who became gentle as Francis began to preach.[56]

human being, and as a Christian. There were no histrionics or miracles, other than the ordinary kind, that day.

Just imagine the flak he received for going—while walking past the crusader troops who were lying in wait for that same Sultan and his men. They were in recuperation mode, as the next battle was a few days away. I imagine scenes from films I've seen about the American Civil War: the sick and the wounded, the "doctors" doing on the spot surgeries by amputating arms and legs. Screaming. Misery. From the late medieval Crusades to the American Civil War, we're talking about pre-modern medicine. Here comes a barefoot little guy with a friend wanting to talk with the enemy about Christ and peace.

Then I see him again, while walking back through their ranks after the meeting with the Sultan was over. They would have been asking why he didn't kill the man. "Preaching" a poor Christ crucified and humiliated, rather than Christ the conquering king, Francis would have seemed as crazy as an old priest making friends with a frog.

—

Find the story: LF 24

Consider a scripture: Jesus said: "You're blessed when your commitment to God provokes persecution. The persecution drives you even deeper into God's kingdom. Not only that—count yourselves blessed every time people put you down or throw you out or speak lies about you to discredit me. What it means is that the truth is too close for comfort and they are uncomfortable. You can be glad when that happens—give a cheer, even!—for though they don't like it, *I* do! And all heaven applauds. And know that you are in good company. My prophets and witnesses have always gotten into this kind of trouble." (Matthew 5:10-12, The Message)

23 Practicing attachment

Talking with birds, loving lambs, caring for lepers, "preaching" to people working in the fields, embracing the ground beneath your feet, are all ways of experiencing God in the way of Saint Francis. They're also ways of attaching yourself to a chosen place in the world, rooting yourself where you are because where you are matters. Matter, in fact, matters a great deal.

In the Christian imagination, this is what Incarnation is about, and Francis' dedication to matter causes him to stand out among his contemporaries as one of the few leaders in the late medieval European Church who taught that our common home is not heaven so much as it is this present Earth. Similarly, in spirituality that is inspired by Francis, the Incarnation of God in Christ took place because of God's love for creation—not to remedy something that sin had caused to happen.

There were many attachments for Francis. In daily life, attachment to his brothers (fellow friars) was a daily routine and a grounding. When he traveled, which was on estimate about half his days as a friar, he was always in the company of his spiritual brothers, and they would continue their practices of prayer and acts of charity wherever they went. They stopped in every small town and established connections there, forming links in a chain, as it were, all over Italy and far beyond. The Franciscan movement thus grew faster than any spiritual movement Europe had witnessed up until that point in history.

But consider one iconic scene in particular: the event, early in Francis' ministry, when he rebuilt the church of San Damiano. Always this story is told (including by me, in past books) as an example of Francis' simplicity and obedience. He hears God telling him: "Go and rebuild my church," so he goes and does that, right away, with bricks and mortar. It is like the irresistible myth of the illiterate Saint Antony from centuries earlier, who was in church one day and heard the Gospel from Matthew chapter nineteen read aloud from the front of the church—"If you want to be perfect, go, sell what you have and give to the poor, and you will have treasures in heaven." Supposedly, he assumed these were words directed at him personally—some commentaries even suggest that he woke from a dead sleep just as they were being read, thinking they were spoken to him personally from God above—and so Antony did what he was told, and left immediately for the desert.

Fifteen years later, when leaders in the Roman church were already considering Francis a saint, they began to return to this story with its account of Francis' obedience, as in, isn't it amazing that he heard those words from God so simply! We now understand that those "words from God" were not intended to be so literally understood; they were prophetic, meaning that this young man would essentially rebuild the whole institution. Yet, his simple response was to gather stones and tools and start working on the walls of San Damiano. How naively beautiful! But there's another way to see it.

This is "the first work he undertook after gaining his freedom from his father," says the earliest account of what happened. His father had just accused his son publicly of theft and disobedience in front of every person in town. Francis had made another one of his iconic gestures: stripping off all his clothes and laying them at his dad's feet, telling him (and everyone who was looking) that now his only father was in heaven. Imagine how painful that had been. Now, imagine how unlikely it would be, if that happened to you, that you'd stay in the city where you were born and raised.

Francis chose to rebuild *that* church—the one where he'd heard the message from God. He could have easily moved along to the next town, where, as it happened in those days, he would have known no one and started all over. But he stayed and faced his vulnerability and day after day worked to rebuild a broken foundation with stones he begged from the same neighbors who had watched him embarrassed by his dad. I can't think of a better example of practicing attachment than this.

He was a man of dramatic gestures: leaping from the horse to kiss that leper, stripping off his clothes in the piazza to make a point; such energy in a charismatic religious figure often leads to a lot of travel to find more and more audiences—rather than staying put and forming attachments. But Francis did the latter to a special degree. He knew the power of place and the importance of staying put and putting down roots.

Kentucky farmer and essayist Wendell Berry writes "[W]hen a community loses its memory, its members no longer know each other. How can they know each other if they have forgotten or have never learned each other's stories? If they do not know each other's stories, how can they know whether or not to trust each other? People who do not trust each other do not help each other, and moreover they fear each other. And this is our predicament now." I see Francis remaining where he was, establishing friaries where his friends would remain where they are, and making slow change for the better into a new pattern.

Wendell Berry concludes that essay with this: "I know that one resurrected rural community would be more convincing and more encouraging than all the government and university programs of the last fifty years.... It would have to be done, not from the outside by the instruction of visiting experts, but from the inside by the ancient rule of neighborliness, by the love of precious things, and by the wish to be at home."[57] By attachment.

Francis had roots, and kept them. And he deepened roots, strengthening them. One of Mary Oliver's beautiful poems begins with the line, "My work is loving the world." She might as well be quoting Francis. Especially as she goes on to praise sunflowers, hummingbirds, bread-making, sheep in pastures, and a torn coat that's far from perfect, with gratitude that "all the ingredients are here."[58]

—

Find the story: TC 18
Consider a scripture: "The river of God is full of water.... The pastures of the wilderness drip, the hills gird themselves with joy, the meadows clothe themselves with flocks, the valleys deck themselves with grain, they shout and sing together for joy." (Psalm 65:9,12-13, RSV)

And remember the first of the "Four Great Vows" recited at the beginning of many Buddhist services: "However innumerable beings are, I vow to save them."[59]

24 Practicing detachment

Meanwhile, *detaching* from matter, stuff, and things is also how Francis experienced God. Finding the permanent amid the changing and circumstantial.

When Francis realized that his purpose was to be actively involved in the affairs of the world (look back at experience #10), he still held onto his contemplative tendencies. Jacques de Vitry, a French theologian who as bishop of Acre (in the kingdom of Jerusalem at that time) in 1216 had occasion to visit Francis and his followers in Assisi, recorded: "During the day they go into cities and villages. They give themselves to activity, reaching out to people, but at night they return to remote and solitary places to devote themselves to contemplation." Sometimes attachment and detachment work together.

I know this may seem odd today—to hold up as exemplary what I am about to hold up—but consider for a moment those iconic occasions when Francis stripped himself naked, or was happy to be naked as he was the moment he was born. There was the time when his religious life began, in front of all the people of Assisi, in the bishop's piazza (just mentioned in #23), his father confronting him, demanding an apology for insolence, and Francis responds—how? By removing his father's clothes, laying them at his dad's feet, and saying, "My only father now is in heaven."

There was also the occasion a couple years later when he

was too severe in ordering his good friend Rufino to go and preach in town, and so Francis finds him and begins to preach himself, but removing all his clothes, to do so in total humility. And at the end of his life wanting to die in the way he was born, he removed his clothes to feel the dirt of the ground on his skin.

Francis remembered that Jesus was stripped naked on the cross, and before that, he was born naked—as were we. And the swaddling clothes of the Gospel account of the Nativity were viewed by Francis as a bookend to the tiny strip of clothing that Christ had on, the night of his humiliating death. So you can see why nakedness was somehow religious to Francis, and how Jesus in the manger was poor and suffering and naked, not cute and chubby and sentimental, as we tend to make him, or see him, in creches today. Francis wants people to see the poverty of the Child who came to be mixed up with the poverty of others, in that manger.

Clare of Assisi, in the Rule she wrote for herself and her Sisters, said: "Out of love of the most holy and beloved Child wrapped in poor swaddling clothes and placed in a manger and of his most holy mother, I admonish, beg, and encourage my sisters to wear poor garments." To wear rough-hewn clothes, then as now, was to live counterculturally, and for Francis and Clare it was to do so in imitation of the king born in a stable.

In Clare's first letter to Agnes (a Bohemian princess who'd become a Poor Clare nun), Clare held up nakedness, just as Francis had done, saying to Agnes "One clothed cannot fight another naked, because she who has something to be caught hold of is more easily thrown to the ground." In other words, one can only fight evil when one is stripped of all attachments and comforts.

Francis detached frequently too, into mystical prayer. Paradoxically, the founder of a religious order of preachers, he was also often alone in profound silence before his God. We've seen that already in these pages—and this aspect of his spirituality was even over-emphasized in the generations and centuries after his death (by Bonaventure, for example) among his direct spiritual inheritors.

Detachment can be for purposes of refreshment and rest, and it is part of the spiritual formation of any would-be monk or friar. Shut up, be quiet, and listen. But detachment is also about identity—remaining focused and centered on who you essentially are. Turning inward, an essential aspect of detachment, is not about turning away from the needs of the world. Detachment moments are not world-denying. Thomas Merton explains this best: "[W]e do not detach ourselves from things in order to attach ourselves to God, but rather we become detached *from ourselves* in order to see and use all things in and for God."[60]

Through detachment—in those caves, or alone at night, or in any number of other places and ways—it is as if Francis was able to remember and meditate on what God had already said and done. This didn't leave him wanting to separate himself from all that is—but gave him the opportunity to listen for what has yet to be. That listening detachment was one of his most regular and repeated experiences of God.

—

Find the story: LF 10, TS 214
Consider a scripture: One effect of Thomas Merton's detachment practice was to see connections: "This leaf has its own texture and its own patterns of veins and its own holy shape, and the bass and trout hiding in the deep pools of the river are canonized by their beauty and their strength. The lakes hidden among the hills are saints, and the sea too is a saint who praises God without interruption in her majestic dance."[61]

And Sōtō Zen master Shunryu Suzuki: "The Lotus Sutra says, to light up one corner of the world—that is enough. Not the whole world. Just make it clear where you are."[62]

25 Overcoming fear

Francis learned to see God in the faces of other people, first by overcoming the fear and revulsion he felt at the sight of those sick and disfigured with leprosy. In his own words he said it was "living in sin" when he was frightened to look at those who were sick, let alone be with them or touch them. And when he "left the world"—again his words—it meant that he had been moved by God to overcome that fear of vulnerability completely. Francis tells the story as if God took the fear away. His first biographer retells it that Francis was "made stronger than himself."

Then, toward the end of his life, he overcame his fear to receive treatment for oncoming blindness. (The treatment likely made it worse, not better, but he didn't know that.) It was this near-blindness that made his poem/song, "Canticle of the Creatures," all the more beautiful, because as he is praising and singing of Sister Moon and the stars, he can no longer really see them. He can feel Brother Wind and Brother Sun without being able to see much of their effects.

I think of the Irish writer James Joyce, whose own vision was seriously impaired, writing in a letter to a friend, "What the eyes bring is nothing. I have a hundred worlds to create, I am losing only one of them."[63]

Then we see Francis talking to Brother Fire. Why did he

choose it, of all the aspects of life to praise as sacred? I suppose it's possible that he knew how Jews, since ancient times, have blessed God, "Sovereign of all worlds, who creates the light of fire" in the *Havdalah* ceremony at the close of every *Shabbat*.

He was remembering something that happened several weeks earlier, when instruments heated by the hot coals of a doctor's fireplace were used to cauterize his eye. He winces with the memory. But then sings this verse:

> Praise God for our Brother Fire,
> through whom you give us light in darkness.
> Brother is bright and pleasant, mighty and strong.

When Francis sang, he encouraged others to sing with him. We've seen mystics of various spiritual traditions over the centuries use prayer and chant in this sort of way and there is a word for it in the religions of the East: Hinduism, Buddhism, Sikhism, Jainism—*samadhi*. It's a compound Sanskrit word that roughly translates as "God-consciousness" or "divine ecstasy." Francis had such experiences, the stigmata chief among them. But we might also imagine his singing in this way. This was no organ accompanied hymn-sing. Like a Hungarian nineteenth-century rebbe, or like Sri Ramakrishna chanting the names of God, I imagine Francis finding a tune between the holy words of his composing and the music of the earth itself.

Was he singing to overcome his fear? Probably. It reminds me of Shadrach, Meshach, and Abednego in the book of Daniel chapter three. They were leaders of the Babylonian province for King Nebuchadnezzar in the sixth century BCE. When the king had a golden statue built and commanded that everyone must worship it, these three would not, so Nebuchadnezzar had them thrown into a furnace. In certain translations (from the Septuagint) we hear this detail: "They walked around in the midst of the flames, singing hymns to God and blessing the Lord."

Only because he first overcame his fear was Francis able to know that holy presence. His consciousness of God and ecstatic communion with the divine were enabled in those moments of becoming stronger than himself.

—

Find the story: TC 17
Consider a scripture: "'Come,' my heart says, 'seek his face!' Your face, LORD, do I seek. Wait for the LORD; be strong, and let your heart take courage; wait for the LORD!" (Psalm 27:8,14 (NRSV)

And a song that Ramakrishna composed and loved to teach his followers was this, very much in the spirit of Saint Francis, with God in the image of the Divine Mother: "Upon the sea of the world unfolds the lotus of the New Day, / And there the Mother sits enshrined in blissful majesty. / See how the bees are mad with joy, sipping the nectar there! / Behold the Mother's radiant face, which so enchants the heart / And captivates the universe! About Her Lotus Feet / Bands of ecstatic holy men are dancing in delight."[64]

26 Getting rid of stuff

In the beginning, Francis knew he wanted a different life from what he'd known in his father's house. *Surely there is more than this.* He was beginning to pray and spend time alone for long periods of time, which was a new experience, but he didn't know what exactly God wanted of him. He couldn't see yet what he was supposed to do.

At mass one day, he heard the Gospel read aloud, and may not have understood it all. The reading would have been done in the ecclesiastical Latin of the thirteenth-century church, and Francis, not having formal education, probably only caught a few essential words. Maybe he heard *Christus... discipulus... pecunia*. Christ... disciples... money. It was enough to suggest that this might be some everyday relevance to whatever was supposed to come next. He stayed after mass that day and asked the priest to explain the Gospel to him, which the priest did "line by line."

But there are also other accounts of how and where and with whom this happened. Another account says that Francis and a friend, who became Brother Bernard, the first to catch the flame started by Francis in Assisi, went together to church asking the priest to help them open the Bible at random (think "random" like a Ouija board), which the priest did, and they landed on three different verses from the gospels.

The readings that day were from the accounts of what Jesus said to the first men who asked what to do to join him in the new sort of life Jesus seemed to be demonstrating around first century Galilee. One was from Matthew's gospel, chapter nineteen, which included: "If you wish to be complete, go sell what you have and give the money to the poor. Then come follow me." In other words, go without planning, without worrying about what you will need tomorrow. Francis did this, and found joy and freedom in it.

He went on to practice this in a variety of ways—on one occasion, for instance, exchanging the new clothes off his back with the ragged clothes of a beggar standing in front of St. Peter's in Rome. As he opened himself to others with all that he had, his worries fell away with his possessions.

This reminds me of a story Thomas Merton tells in one of his last books, about a farmer: "One evening he heard some noise in the garden. He noticed a young man of the village atop a tree stealing his fruit. Quietly, he went to the shed where he kept his ladder and took it under the tree so that the intruder might safely make his descent. He went back to his bed unnoticed. The farmer's heart, emptied of self and possession, could not think of anything else but the danger that might befall the young village delinquent."[65]

You could say that the concept of "owning" things is an illusion anyway. Everything in the world is connected and interconnected. Francis seems to have understood the world like this, which is why not owning things was effortless for him. (It wasn't just that he was doing his duty, following a rule set by his teacher.) He didn't feel the necessity to hold onto anything.

Again, I like how Shunryu Suzuki taught it: "Our effort in Zen is to observe everything as-it-is. Yet even though we say so, we are not necessarily observing everything as-it-is. We say, 'Here is my friend, over there is the mountain, and way up there is the moon.' But your friend is not only your friend, the mountain is not only the mountain, and the moon is not only the moon. If we think, 'I am here and the mountain is over there,' that is a dualistic way of observing things. To go to San Francisco, we have to cross over the Tassajara mountains. That is our usual understanding. But that is not the Buddhist way of observing things. We find the mountain or the moon or our friend or San Francisco within ourselves. Right here. That is big mind within which everything exists."[66]

So forget for a moment that Jesus commanded that all his disciples get rid of stuff and move about the world unencumbered. Instead, consider how this way of rejecting the values of the world became for Francis more than any other single practice, a way of experiencing God by emptying the self of expectations.

—

Find the story: TC 22, 24; BO 3.1,3 and 1.6
Consider a scripture: "Therefore I tell you, do not worry about your life, what you will eat or what you will drink, or about your body, what you will wear. Is not life more than food, and the body more than clothing? Look at the birds of the air..." (Matthew 6:25-26, NRSV)

And "Be empty of worrying / Think of who created thought / Why do you stay in prison / When the door is wide open?" (Rumi)[67]

27 Looking to dreams

Let's be honest: Saint Francis and his insistence on doing the impossible—being loving, gentle, and peaceful all the time, and resourceful without money—can be frustrating. No one can live up to the perfection asked by Jesus in the Sermon on the Mount, teachings that Francis attempted to follow to the letter.

This is one reason why, starting about twenty-five years after Francis' death we have evidence of people turning on the Franciscans. There arose then what's called "antifraternalism" (*anti*, against + *fraternalism*, mendicant religious orders). The once-poor Franciscans were now rather wealthy; the once simple and austere friars were now often chubby or even drunk in public. So people turned on them. This included physical assaults. Geoffrey Chaucer of *The Canterbury Tales* was one such instigator. According to *The New Oxford Book of Literary Anecdotes*, Chaucer personally beat up a Franciscan on Fleet Street in London, which explains the disdain he shows for friars in his famous book as well.

But Francis was about much more than "Be ye therefore perfect"—yes, Jesus actually said that.* Francis' life was about embracing things. This included what today we call the subconscious—that powerful, often unknown and untapped source

*Matthew 5:48, KJV

within of feelings, emotions, past action and history, with the power to influence us in the present.

A good therapist today may help someone remember, recall, and find meaning in their nighttime dreaming. A therapist will help you see, hear, taste, and smell it again, to pay attention to the details that arise, and the feelings they give rise to. We have to pay attention to these hidden parts of ourselves because what's hidden is much more than what is easily seen. As Korean philosopher Byung-Chul Han says: "I am not at all transparent to myself. The conscious within our psyche is very small. It is surrounded by broad dark edges."[68] That's surely right. Well, Francis did this 800 years ago.

At critical moments, he awoke in the morning with a dream (often called a "vision" in the literature) he remembered and through which he discovered something of himself. The first time we're told this took place was when Francis woke up questioning the choice he and his father had made pointing him toward life as a knight. "Trying to avoid the divine grasp," explains Francis' first biographer, he joined a campaign to fight Apulia with other noblemen seeking fame and fortune. God visited Francis during the night, it says. Francis saw in the dream a great gathering of wealth—everything he'd been desiring—and so he arose delighted, feeling that he was about to be a great success.

Only to realize a few hours later that he hadn't understood the dream at all. He knew this because he was receptive to his feelings, such that it dawned on him that he felt unmoved by that vision of material and soldierly glory. The things he saw in the dream were glittery, but he was to look past them. He realized he wanted something else entirely, and that the dream was in fact pointing him away from what was unimportant.

This is the occasion when Francis seems to have been a deserter from a field of impending battle. To leave at such a moment took great courage. He would have known that he was going to be criticized, ostracized, maybe even arrested. But he turned and left in pursuit of what really mattered to him.

Years later, when Francis is alone on the mountain of La Verna and has his experience that we now call receiving the stigmata—the same word, "vision," is used to describe what he saw and what happened to and with him during the night—but it may be that "dream" is the best translation from the Italian. For even while it's said that the stigmata wounds were imprinted upon his flesh, Francis was there "unable to decide what this vision meant for him."

That is the work of dreaming—being receptive and prepared to receive messages from the holy places God inhabits, and listening to what they mean for our lives.

Another instance we know of, in Francis' life, was on the eve of his visiting the pope in Rome, asking for his approval of the spiritual movement Francis had underway, with less than a dozen companions. Francis was nervous and anxious and he understood the dream as a message from the Spirit of God, meant to comfort him. That meeting with the pope went well, but a decision in Francis' favor didn't come right away. The pope said, we'll think and pray on it (that's the royal "we")—and it was in a dream of his own that Innocent III saw the answer, which he took as if from God, to bless Francis' efforts.

—

Find the story: TC 1.5-6, 94; BO 3.8-10

Consider a scripture: "When Joseph came to them in the morning, he saw that they were troubled. So he asked Pharaoh's officers, who were with him in custody in his master's house, 'Why are your faces downcast today?' They said to him, 'We have had dreams, and there is no one to interpret them.' And

Joseph said to them, 'Do not interpretations belong to God? Please tell them to me.'" (Genesis 40:6-8, NRSV)

And remember what Albert Einstein said: "Curiosity has its own reason for existing. We cannot help but be in awe when we contemplate the mysteries of eternity, of life, of the marvelous structure of reality. It is enough if one tries merely to comprehend a little of this mystery every day. Never lose a holy curiosity."[69]

28 Returning home

There are so many stories of spiritual pilgrims who visit far-off places to find their true purpose. It's as if they discover a piece of the puzzle of their lives wherever they go, and then finally put the whole thing together. This formula is so tried and apparently true that it remains the pattern for many a best-selling spiritual memoir.

The story of Siddhartha Guatama (the Buddha) is like this. Born in Nepal, he became a wandering ascetic and eventually found enlightenment under the bodhi tree in India. Mohandas Gandhi was born in Porbandar, in the west of India, but he left to go to England and study, and then South Africa to practice law for more than two decades, before realizing he was destined to do his life's work back at home in India. Jesus Christ is a bit like this too: born in Bethlehem, we don't see him going back there ever again, and he only returns to Nazareth, where he was raised, once—and the reception was unwelcome.

For most famous religious teachers, where they were born and grew up is a long way from where they realize themselves. It is common for a person to leave home, when given the opportunity, to seek new opportunities. Especially in the lives of religious and spiritual figures who have had a large impact. They often find life's meaning in another place entirely from the one that they originally called home. And when they don't have the opportunity to do this, they feel stuck.

You sometimes can't see yourself properly in an old, familiar place. And people can't see the real you.

Francis was born in Assisi, partied in Assisi, had an emotional breakdown in Assisi, was abused by his father in Assisi, did some crazy talking with birds in Assisi, and mocked by former friends in Assisi, all before becoming a saint. The point is, he underwent it all in the same place. When he left Assisi, it was always in order to come back again. And one reason why we have stories of him being mocked is because the proverb is true: a prophet/or mensch/or saint is rarely recognized as such in his own country.

For example, when Francis failed as a minor crusader, was imprisoned, and later deserted, he gave back the "saddles, shields, spears, and other equipment" that his biographer mentions—he never really used them anyway—and returned home. And when he changed his way of life, replacing fine living with ragged clothes and begging for food, he also stayed nearby. He did all of this in front of the people who had known him since he was a baby. Imagine what people in Assisi must have said to his parents. "What's wrong with Francis?" "I'm sorry about your boy."

It was in church one day, after hearing the Gospel readings with Jesus urging his disciples to live with poverty and not worry about tomorrow, that the text says Francis said: "This is what I want. This is what I seek, this is what I desire with all my heart." And his biographer adds, "The holy father, overflowing with joy, hastened to implement the words of salvation, and did not delay before he devoutly began to put into effect what he heard."

If I'd received a revelation from God like that, and radically changed my life, I would have done it in a place well-suited to starting over. Even more to the point, it is difficult for me to imagine having any revelation whatsoever if I were still living in the town where I was raised. I'm one of those people who go elsewhere seeking enlightenment. Instead, Francis found that, rather than "starting over," which is often a form of escapism, it was in fact the act of returning and returning again, which brought him into a place of deeper realization of God.

In some traditions (particularly Judaism), this sense of "returning" is what one does in response to sin. Also, to face the dark parts of ourselves. This returning is called *teshuvah* in Hebrew, meaning "return" and "repentance" both. Rabbi Adina Allen speaks of it this way: "Rather than turning away from our human failings, teshuvah beckons us toward these complicated, as of yet unintegrated places within."[70] I'm not sure if Francis was doing that on purpose—by always coming back home, even when things went terribly wrong—but it is the effect of what he did in doing so. It made him more whole.

It takes courage to do so.

How much easier that path could have been if he had been able to start over, or refine himself, somewhere else. But one gets the sense that the opposite is actually true: to experience God, Francis needed to undergo it all without hiding, invention, or the ability to create personae. That's what we mean when we say, to experience God you should be willing—may need to in fact—return to where you began. You can't get closer to God without getting close to yourself.

—

Find the story: TC 5, 22

Consider a scripture: "How lovely is your dwelling place, O Lord of hosts! My soul longs, indeed it faints, for the courts of the Lord; my heart and my flesh sing for joy to the living God. Even the sparrow finds a home and the swallow a nest for herself, where she may lay her young, at your altars, O Lord of hosts, my King and my God. Happy are those who live in your house, ever singing your praise." (Psalm 84:1-4, NRSV)

"How noble and good everyone could be if, every evening before falling asleep, they were to recall to their minds the events of the whole day and consider exactly what had been good and bad. Then, without realizing it, you try to improve yourself at the start of each new day. Of course, you achieve quite a lot in the course of time. Anyone can do this. It costs nothing and is certainly very helpful. Whoever doesn't know it must learn and find by experience that: 'A quiet conscience makes one strong.'" (Anne Frank)[71]

29 Sleeping in abandoned churches

I never promised that all of these thirty-six ways would be easy to emulate. Well, perhaps I did. This one may be the exception.

We get the sense that Francis found God where others had abandoned God. His religious commitments began when he was spending time in the dilapidated church of San Damiano (see #19), and when he asked a bishop for permission to use the lonely Portiuncula chapel (#20).

He was often looking for ruined churches where he might pray—and spend the night. We saw earlier his preference for praying in the dead of night. I think of him here like the psalmist praying at night when she said, "I think of God, and I moan.... I am so troubled that I cannot speak" (Psalm 77:3-4, RSV). Finding ruined churches and spending time there wasn't unheard of, prior to Francis—there were a lot of church ruins throughout Europe in the early thirteenth century—but it was uncommon for the founders of religious orders to do this.

Remember how he loved the nighttime, so gaps in the roof above his head were just fine. We know, in fact, that Francis very often slept in the open air, and that he disapproved of friars building permanent houses for their use.

On this occasion, he was walking with Brother Pacifico, who was known to love to sing, when Francis said, "Let's go to Saint Peter of Bovara. I would like to stay there tonight." Everyone knew that St. Peter's in the tiny village of Bovara, a hamlet just outside of Trevi, sat empty. Trevi had been destroyed by war and not yet rebuilt. The people of Trevi and Bovara, and even their priest, were mostly gone.*

Only the hospital in Trevi had people there, and that is where Pacifico spent the night. Meanwhile, Francis said his Compline prayers in the abandoned church and then settled down to sleep, but couldn't. He experienced temptation while lying down to sleep, and so he went outside the church, crossed himself, and asked God to take the temptation away. This happened, and Francis then went back inside and slept peacefully. When Pacifico returned to the church the following morning he found Francis standing in the choir, facing the altar.

This is another way that Francis experienced God—and not by talking. He wasn't what my wife calls "frontal," as in the frontal lobe that feeds personalities, often male, who spend a lot of energy teaching, organizing, scheming, debating, justifying, and generally telling everyone what they think. I like how Paulo Freire, the Brazilian educator criticized this as "the banking method" when he was trying to reform educational practices. It was once a common assumption that any leader or teacher was supposed to simply "deposit" information with his listeners.

Such frontal activities were of little importance to Francis. I like how the modern biographer Paul Sabatier puts this: "A great part of St. Francis' power came to him through his systematic avoidance of polemics [which] is always more or less a form of spiritual pride. It only deepens the chasm that it undertakes to fill up. Truth needs not to be proved; it is its own witness."[72] Francis' witness was always his lifestyle—a life of spiritual practice.

Sleeping in abandoned churches happens in Paulo Coelho's

*There is to this day a Chiesa di San Pietro, Bovara.

novel, *The Alchemist*, with a shepherd named Santiago who, together with his flock of sheep, tries it. In one scene in one of these churches, a sycamore has grown in precisely the room where the sacristy (a small room adjacent the sanctuary where a priest prepares for mass) once stood. Beautiful symbolism.

I've also seen Reddit and Tumblr pages devoted to tips for exploring abandoned churches. Advice that was given included "If you have to sleep there, sleep in the sanctuary, but not on a pew." (Uncomfortable, I guess?) "If you go alone, don't bring a flashlight. You'll see things you don't want to." (The gothic vibe is real.) And "If you hear the organ playing, your time is up." (Like I said.)

Both 800 years ago and now, an abandoned church is a powerful symbol of lost power, vacated faith, vanishing hope. Let's be honest: it can also be a symbol of bankruptcy and scandal. Francis of Assisi is sometimes claimed by Holy Mother Church as her most faithful son, and I'm not so sure that's true—because he was often anti-institutional in subtle ways—but it is certainly true that Francis wanted to bring the hope of religion back into the lives of people who had left it behind. In that way, and because thousands of churches close every year now in the United States alone, Francis' life and teachings are as relevant today as they were then.

So this example of experiencing God may be odd, or difficult, to follow today, but I expect some of us will find a way.

—

Find the story: AC 65

Consider a scripture: "Hear the word of the LORD.... 'He who scattered Israel will gather him and will keep him as a shepherd does a flock.' For the LORD has ransomed Jacob and has redeemed him from hands too strong for him. They shall come and sing aloud on the height of Zion, and they shall be radiant over the goodness of the LORD, over the grain, the wine, and the oil, and over the young of the flock and the herd; their life shall become like a watered garden, and they shall never languish again. Then shall the young women rejoice in the dance, and the young men and the old shall be merry. I will turn their mourning into joy." (Jeremiah 31:10-13, NRSV)

30 Turning emotions into actions

"When I dare to be powerful, to use my strength in the service of my vision, then it becomes less and less important whether I am afraid," said the Black writer Audre Lorde. Never one to keep his feelings bottled up, Francis would tell both friends and the powerful what pained him, tempted and troubled him. And in those places he frequented, he'd talk with God about such things. His passions rose to the surface, always, and his life was like a flooding stream.

On one occasion, a temptation wouldn't leave him such that he lost his usual joy and affability. Life felt very dark to him then. This in fact went on for almost two years until one day while kneeling in the Portiuncula he remembered a teaching of Jesus: "Truly I tell you, if you say to this mountain, 'Be taken up and thrown into the sea,' and if you do not doubt in your heart but believe that what you say will come to pass, it will be done for you" (Mark 11:23). He knew then that his temptation was that mountain, and he became free of it.

Before this happened, when he turned to face that leper on the road, Francis had eyes filled with disgust. His father and the church had taught him that the world was a fair place, organized such that some people were fortunate and some were not, some were deserving of health and happiness, and some not. This prejudice became like a mountain thrown into the sea, sanctified and unquestioned. Until.

Philosopher Martha Nussbaum has observed that emotions can be like "upheavals of thought," when our assumptions are shattered—and then we do something to show it.[73] This is emotions turning into actions. When Francis jumped off his horse, ran, and embraced that leper on the road—and wept—he was sharing an emotional upheaval that involved action. He was stirred up. I think he knew that it was good to be stirred up, and to put himself in positions where he'd be likely to be stirred.

We may love the calm, but we need storms. Francis then became someone for whom the wounds of the world were carried by him, in him. For the rest of his days, he responded to the poor "wanting to give them not only his possessions but his very self," Bonaventure tells us. This is an exhausting way to live, but for certain special people there is no other way. Perhaps you know someone like this. I do. They feel the wounds of others so keenly that they can almost never again feel comfortable.

Most of us cope differently—with a bit of distance and rationalization. As James Baldwin writes in *Another Country*: "How can you live if you can't love? And how can you live if you do?"

If you think of the occasions when you may have wept in the past, these may have been moments of either separation from, or reunion with, someone to whom you are intimately connected. Francis' weeping on the leper's neck was both of these.

Which isn't to suggest that then everything became clear to him. Darkness and confusion fill us much of the time, even though we deny it, and Francis was no different. I like that about him too. At the end of his life, one can read his quiet suffering from various physical ailments, as well as disappointment in how his own religious order is changing, as a kind of sadness. I think it's much more than that. I think we see Francis at the end of life returning to, and remembering, the origins of his quest for God, which began in dark places. He felt comfortable in dark spaces because they didn't "get him down" so much as they were like water and soil for seeds of what was good.

The late Zen teacher Thich Nhat Hanh used to offer a spiritual practice which fits beautifully here. It is such a practical way to turn emotions and passions, that are sometimes entirely private, into actions that make a difference for those around us: "Arrange things in your daily life so that you have time to water your positive seeds. Ask your loved ones to practice in the same way. Say, 'Darling, if you really care for me, please water the good seeds in me every day. I am capable of loving, understanding, and forgiving and I need your help to practice these in my daily life. I promise to recognize the positive seeds in you, as well, and to do my best to water them every day.' This is true love."[74]

But my favorite anecdote about this kind of active hope and dedication to practice comes from the Jewish tradition. In one of the tractates of the Talmud it says, "If you have a sapling in your hand when people tell you the messiah has come, first plant the sapling, then go out to greet him" (*Avot d'Rabbi Natan*). The only thing that's ever changed the world for good is practice—and practice is prompted by emotions in the way of Francis.

—

Find the story: AC 63, BO 1.6
Consider a scripture: "Set me as a seal upon your heart, as a seal upon your arm; for love is strong as death, passion fierce as the grave. Its flashes are flashes of fire, a raging flame. Many waters cannot quench love, neither can floods drown it. If one offered for love all the wealth of one's house, it would be utterly scorned." (Song of Songs 8:6-7, NRSV)

31 Giving away what you really don't need

It might be impossible for us to be satisfied living with as little as Francis did. But the principle of his frugality and generosity was this: What we have is on loan to us.

This is why, when meeting a poor man on the road near Siena, he gave him his coat, saying to a companion who was with him that day: "We need to return this coat to the one to whom it belongs." The companion argued with Francis, concerned that he would now be too cold. But Francis said, "After meeting him, I see that keeping that coat would make me a thief." He experienced joy in this, because to him money and possessions most often brought misery and unhappiness.

He had a point. This is still often true.

In the early days when Francis was still rebuilding churches with stones, he was mostly alone in the work, just doing what he thought God told him. He was walking around like a hermit, carrying a staff, as his early biographers tell us. "One day the gospel was being read in that church about how the Lord sent out his disciples to preach. Francis, who was attending there, in order to understand better the words, humbly begged the priest after celebrating the solemnities of the mass to explain the gospel to him. Once the priest explained it all, Francis said, 'This is what I want and what I seek and desire with all my heart.'"

It was a turning point. From that moment on, Francis kept it very simple. He even jettisoned the fancy staff—imagine a nicely carved walking stick that proclaimed *I am such a pious hermit* to all who passed him on the street; he didn't need that anymore. His poverty went from a little bit of performance to a quieter form of detachment. This is also why the earliest Franciscans were known not so much for the brown color of their cloaks as for their very drab color, because Francis did then what today we would call reusing whatever secondhand material was available. The friars' clothes didn't match except in that they were all similarly unattractive.

So yes, Francis famously gave all his stuff away, and instructed anyone who wanted to follow him in his way of life to do similarly. He did this because it's what Jesus taught: that it is in poverty that we know God, identify with God in Christ, and do our duty as people of faith. The most memorable scenes, rarely shown in the movies or told in the books about Francis, are of the first friars disposing of their stuff as Francis waits nearby to be sure that they've done so completely.

Is that what we are supposed to do still today? When Jesus in the gospels told a young man the first step to discovering the will of God—"If you wish to be perfect, go, sell your possessions, and give the money to the poor, and you will have treasure in heaven; then come, follow me" (Mt. 19:21)—he did it with the first disciples in earshot. The following verse is then one of the saddest of all: "When the young man heard this word, he went away grieving, for he had many possessions."

As any student of early Franciscan history and theology knows, this issue—the ownership of property, stuff, and keeping of money—became the most divisive point among Franciscans, pitting friars against each other in the century after Francis' death. It even led to Pope John XXII officially opposing Francis' teaching on poverty, ruling in a papal bull of 1323 that it was heretical to say Christ and the apostles owned nothing, carried no money, and other teachings that Francis had earlier made explicit.[75]

But what's often misunderstood is how, for Francis, giving away what you don't need was not about penance for sins, or any form of guilt for having when others don't. It was most of all about freedom. Turn back to the first way of experiencing God we saw in this book—and the drawing opposite the title page of that bird escaping its cage to fly into the sky. To have unnecessary stuff was to then have worries about keeping and protecting it, and all of that inevitably always leads to wanting more. And more. Francis had that soaring freedom feeling of holy air under his wings when he gave away what he didn't need.

—

Find the story: AC 32, TC 22
Consider a scripture: "Jesus said to them, 'I am the bread of life. Whoever comes to me will never be hungry, and whoever believes in me will never be thirsty.'" (John 6:35, NRSV)

And Dorothy Day, from the postscript of her autobiography, *The Long Loneliness*: "We cannot love God unless we love each other, and to love we must know each other. We know Him in the breaking of bread, and we know each other in the breaking of bread, and we are not alone any more. Heaven is a banquet and life is a banquet, too, even with a crust, where there is companionship. We have all known the long loneliness and we have learned that the only solution is love and that love comes with community."

32 Being foolish on purpose

When others begin following Francis, doing what he is doing, and a small religious movement begins to form, people urge Francis to adopt what's called a Rule of Life. Look to St. Benedict's Rule, or St. Augustine's, or St. Bernard's constitutions for monastic life, they told him.

"The Lord wants me to be a new kind of fool in the world," Francis answered, adding that he wouldn't become a monk, or simply take on an existing Rule. As a way of experiencing God, this foolishness became a kind of abandonment. A carefree-ness with regard to the planning and organizing that other religious orders might do. It was intended as a rejection of the world's way of doing—wielding power, grabbing what you can for yourself, none of which has changed since Francis' day—in favor of something radically alternative. We call this eccentric behavior, and the word is spot on, because "eccentric" means literally ex-centric. Way outside the center, on the margins.

Going even deeper, and more personally, this new foolishness meant being willing—even pleased—when people look upon you as ridiculous, irrelevant, or useless. So in those early years there were no Franciscan colleges, or friars going off to seminary, or even friar-cooks planning a menu for a meal that might take place tomorrow. Francis even asked his friends to consider not becoming priests unless it was absolutely necessary. They lived entirely in the present, even when it made them appear foolish.

Francis reveled in people finding him silly, feeling that he was closer to God when being ridiculed as God's Son once was. Jesus was a fool, by any worldly Roman standard of his day. And when Francis was among powerful people, he played the fool too. In palaces, courts, and with the powerful, it was often the hired fool who was dressed unconventionally, juggling or playing instruments, who could make jokes at the expense of the mighty. A common person wouldn't dare say things that a fool could say with impunity. A fool flouted convention, poked fun at niceties, and got away with it because he was either feebleminded or very clever. In some scenes with Francis (and his friend, Brother Juniper), it is difficult to distinguish the two.

For example, before there were Franciscan friars in every town in Italy there was a strange method Francis created to spread the word about what their work was about. One friar would go there to visit and sit in the public square all day long, and then for days on end, looking like what came to be known as a Franciscan fool: unshaven, not well-bathed, patched secondhand clothing, and an odd, incongruous smile on his face. "Who are you, and why are you here?" someone would finally ask. Which is when he would pull from his pocket the radically simple Rule of life that the first Franciscans lived by, and share it with them. Within days, we are told, there would be converts to their way of life in that place.

Francis also knew foolishness unintentionally, a gift he still managed to cultivate. In as much as he lived fully in the present, Francis was bound to be seen a fool—and benefit from the simplicity and joy that comes from such foolish living.

Pablo d'Ors, a Spanish Catholic priest who also teaches Zen meditation, recently reflected: "It has cost me four decades to comprehend that people begin to live to the degree to which they quit dreaming of themselves.... Just as the child who is learning to ride a bicycle falls to the ground when they stop to consider how well or poorly they are riding, and actually manages to ride it when they are most deeply submerged in the activity, so are we, all of us, best when submerged in any activity that we undertake."[76]

What we call "holy fools" are those who understand this, and Francis was among them experiencing the holy presence in foolishness.

—

Find the story: AC 18, 52
Consider a scripture: "The message about the cross is foolishness to those who are perishing, but to us who are being saved it is the power of God. For it is written, 'I will destroy the wisdom of the wise, and the discernment of the discerning I will thwart.' Where is the one who is wise? Where is the scribe? Where is the debater of this age? Has not God made foolish the wisdom of the world? For since, in the wisdom of God, the world did not know God through wisdom, God decided, through the foolishness of our proclamation, to save those who believe." (1 Corinthians 1:18-21, NRSV)

33 Keeping holy words in your heart

Can anyone really say what prayer is, does, or means? These questions are unanswerable, except that, for people who pray, when they pray, the questions tend to fall away.

I'll always remember learning centering prayer with M. Basil Pennington, who later became my friend. He was one of the three Trappist monks who brought Centering Prayer to a non-monastic audience beginning in the early 1970s. He's also the one of the three who wrote a *New York Times* best-selling book about it (called simply *Centering Prayer*, published by Doubleday in 1980). Dom Basil would ask everyone to sit comfortably and attentively and to clear their minds of thoughts and preoccupations. To just sit in silence. When a thought arises (and they do, always), just "greet" it, then let it go away. Everyone would then try this, and when the group would come out of twenty minutes of practice Basil would ask for questions. Someone would say, "I'm not sure what I'm doing when I do this." Someone else would ask, "What should I be thinking about as I do this?" Basil would remark, very kindly, "That's perfectly okay." And "Nothing at all."

I've heard friends talk about learning zazen (Zen sitting meditation) with Shunryu Suzuki at Tassajara, and it seems to mirror my contemplative Catholic experience. "What am I supposed to *do*?" one student asked. Another, "I just don't understand." Suzuki Roshi would simply remind them to sit, that the sitting was the point, not what might be "received" while sitting. He'd say "Try not to think so much" and Zen was "nothing special, just sitting, sipping a cup of tea," and he meant it.[77] Dom Basil may have learned his way of teaching from masters of Eastern traditions. I don't know if he had direct experience with Suzuki Roshi, but I know that he did with certain experts in Transcendental Meditation in the sixties.

Evelyn Underhill wrote a century ago, "Prayer is the substance of eternal life," by which she meant that it's a mystical participation in something beyond ourselves. Prayer, Underhill learned from late medieval English mystics, is an intercourse between God and human beings—it moves mysteriously in both directions—and it's part of eternity because it is not so much something observed (as in, *Look, I'm praying now!*) "but emerges unperceived from that deep ground of being where we do not know ourselves apart from [God]."[78]

This is also prayer as Francis understood it.

When Francis pleaded with a young novice not to go and acquire his own breviary (prayer book), at first he argued, "Don't be like those friars who desire knowledge over virtue." When this didn't work, he pleaded, "A prayer book will make you feel like a lord or bishop, and you will say, 'Someone bring me my prayer book!'" And when that didn't work, he begged—running after the younger man, and asking him to stop and listen. Then Francis pointed to the novice's chest and cried, "*There* is your prayer book! *There* is your prayer book!"

Francis was a person of his era, when ordinary people had memory skills and stores superior to ours, so in one sense it was easier for him to keep scripture passages, prayers, and poems in his memory. To know them by heart. But aside from the difference between then and now, it is still possible to experience God in this way—as memorized holy words rise to our minds at times when we most need them.

He didn't write guidelines to prayer, like other famous saints did. He wrote very little, in fact. But in one of the few letters we have from Francis, he's writing to Anthony of Padua, one of the young theologians in their religious order, who's asking permission to teach the other brothers theology. Francis responds: "I am happy that you want to teach sacred theology to the brothers, but please, as it says in our Rule, don't do anything in a way that would extinguish the spirit of prayer and devotion in them." This is a warning that's easily disregarded, as people wanting to experience God try to do so by studying theology instead of becoming people of prayer.

That warning was heeded by Anthony of Padua, but then Anthony died in 1231. Soon, then, the Franciscan approach to studying theology—as well as toward wealth, power, and other things—changed so much that in less than a generation there were friars who were masters of theological colleges at the University of Paris. And by 1256 there was enough influence of friar-scholars in Paris to create a rift between them and the majority of other theologians there. The leader of the Paris opposition, William of Saint-Armour, said the friars were "worse than the Devil, for, while the latter proposed to turn stones into bread [referring to Jesus' encounter with the devil in Matthew chapter 4], the former were already turning poor people's bread into the stone of their fine churches." William accused the friars of pretending to be humble and simple while being politically conniving and arrogant.[79] He wasn't necessarily wrong. This was when Francis' inheritors were also building massive Gothic churches, including the celebrated one in Assisi where they buried their founder.[80]

Francis never really understood what others found so appealing about study and books. Holy words were, for him, something for the heart to treasure and keep. And then, from the heart, those words were supposed to mold a character, guide actions. How naïve this must have sounded to those who came after Francis and never had the experience of walking beside him.

It was enough for him to keep holy words in his heart. It was enough, because he experienced God in doing so.

—

Find the story: AC 103-6
Consider a scripture: "Surely, this commandment that I am commanding you today is not too hard for you, nor is it too far away. It is not in heaven, that you should say, 'Who will go up to heaven for us and get it for us so that we may hear it and observe it?' Neither is it beyond the sea, that you should say, 'Who will cross to the other side of the sea for us and get it for us so that we may hear it and observe it?' No, the word is very near to you; it is in your mouth and in your heart for you to observe." (Deuteronomy 30:11-14, NRSV)

34 Singing to death

Ancient culture knew nothing of silent reading. Reading was done out loud. This is why the verb often translated as "meditate" in Psalm 1:2 really means mumble or "say quietly." We've been reading and understanding it incorrectly all these years. In fact, *Brown-Driver-Briggs* (the standard Hebrew-English lexicon of the Old Testament) translates that Hebrew root, הגה, as "moan" or "growl inarticulately." So, the next time you read Psalm 1:1-2, hear it this way: "Happy are those who...delight... in the law of the Lord, and on his law moan, mumble, and groan day and night."

We moan and groan all the way to the end of life.

I was on retreat recently at the Abbey of Gethsemani in Kentucky, where Thomas Merton was a monk and where his body is buried. Visiting his hermitage in the woods during Advent, I pulled a volume of his journals down from a shelf and read what he wrote on Christmas day 1965: "The midnight Mass...was decent, and I was glad to be there.... I did not get the awful depression that I have had a couple of times at Christmas in recent years. Thank God for that! Perhaps this comes from my thinking about death that has opened out with the last days of Advent—seeing death as built into my life and accepting it in and with life (not trying to push it out of life, keep it away from contaminating a life supposedly completely other than it. Death is flowering in my life as a part and fulfillment of it—its term, its final chord)."[81] I was moved by this, as if Merton were speaking for me too.

Francis felt that one can be close to God in life, and then just as clearly and continuously, in death. He spoke often of reflecting on his death, while alive, and as he aged and suffered from serious illnesses, he began to praise death as part of God's creation, and to sing to it. Francis called death his sister, and he welcomed her. More than once he said, "I am so closely united with my Lord that, in God's mercy, we will be just as united in death."

When Francis was composing his "Canticle of the Creatures," praising Mother Earth and the wind and stars and creatures, he was also at the end of his life. The final verse of that famous song, then, makes room for death. Praises death, even. Francis can hardly open his eyes by this point, and any sunlight is painful to him.

"Come on Brother Ass, you need to get up and get me moving!" I have him say out loud, lying in the garden at Clare's San Damiano convent, where she was caring for him while he wrote and sang, in that play I wrote and performed recently. This is how Francis often referred to his body—comparing it to a beast of burden that never quite does what its master requires of it—with a combination of reverence and frustration in his infirmities. But Francis transforms his discomfort into praise for those parts of earthly existence that most challenge him.

The moment comes several weeks after those first verses of the "Canticle" were written, when he is told by his doctor and friends that his infirmities are beyond healing. The time has come to look forward to death. He does in fact look forward to it. He's come to see life and death as one. Shunryu Suzuki puts this beautifully when he says: "Our life and death are the same thing. When we realize this fact we have no fear of death anymore, and we have no actual difficulty in our life."[82]

"Brother Leo, Brother Angelo, I'm glad that you are here. Stay by my side and sing to me of Sister Death," Francis says in my play. And those brothers—great friends—are puzzled by such a strange request. Who is Francis even talking about? But Francis, then, with friends by his side, composes the final verse in which he praises how a human life comes to an end: "Praise to you, O God, for our Sister Death and the death of the body from whom no one may escape," adding again a few lines later, "Praise to you, O God, and all blessing. We give you thanks and serve you with great humility. Amen."

This was not the "die now, live later" of so much religious teaching. This was a paean of praise to death at the conclusion of having fervently lived.

The Indian fifteenth-century poet Kabir, whose verse became important to Hindu Bhakti as well as Sikh scripture, is sometimes compared to Francis. Like Francis, Kabir rejected the world-renouncing spirituality of the monasticism of his day. Kabir embraced the created world when others said that being spiritual was to deny it. He wrote: "In the home is the true union ... why should I forsake my home and wander in the forest?" And "the home helps to attain Him Who is real. So stay where you are, and all things shall come to you in time."[83]

Death was part of home to Francis. To use Merton's phrase, "death is flowering" in Francis' life in more ways than one, here at the end. May we all find a blooming in our ending.

—

Find the story: AC 99-100
Consider a scripture: "The heart of the wise is in the house of mourning; but the heart of fools is in the house of mirth. Better is the end of a thing than its beginning; and the patient in spirit is better than the proud in spirit. Say not, 'Why were

the former days better than these?' For it is not from wisdom that you ask this. Consider the work of God; who can make straight what he has made crooked? In the day of prosperity be joyful, and in the day of adversity consider; God has made the one as well as the other, so that man may not find out anything that will be after him." (Ecclesiastes 7:4,8,10,13,14)

35 Telling the truth

Looking back at the iconic moments we've remembered, most were occasions when Francis didn't look the other way or smooth things over. That scene in front of his father and the bishop of Assisi, when he took off all his clothes and said what he said—that must have been difficult. Or when he talked with the people of Gubbio while brokering the deal with the wolf who was hurting their citizens—that was Francis telling it like it was, reminding the townspeople of their responsibility to care for everyone, including a hungry wolf.

But there's another scene that we haven't yet looked at, and in it we see this way of experiencing God close-up in Francis. We return to the role of "preaching" in his life. Whether with actions of actual words, the little man, we are told, was always communicating, not doctrine, but God's spirit.

The scene is when Francis and his eleven companions have just returned from visiting Pope Innocent III and the papal curia, and have received permission to keep doing what they've been doing. Everywhere he goes, bolstered with some confidence, Francis is said to be "a preacher of the truth." Contemporaries of Francis, and famous saint-preachers who followed after him, were often praised for their eloquence of speech and exposition of Christian doctrine. The chroniclers give us almost the exact opposite about Francis: "Not in persuasive words of wisdom," it says, "and not with beautiful modes of speech." Interestingly, when they talk about this preaching of truth in him, they speak not of audiences hanging on Francis' words—in fact, he's rarely quoted—but of people "clinging to Francis' footsteps."

Preaching the truth was, for Francis, a way of life, not speech or ideas. He was forthright in what he said, and what he said was consistently shown in what he did.

There was the time, also right after he and his early friends had come back from Rome, when they had their first gathering as a group to discuss the direction of their new spiritual movement. There were many things that Francis sought to fix and correct. The histories tell us that Francis did so—guiding his brothers deliberately and often in fine detail. They use words like "admonish" frequently to describe what Francis did in reminding the others of the promising they'd made and the commitments they needed to keep.

But to be sure he was truthful, Francis asked for one of their number to "be his guardian and master." To watch him, to see what he does when others aren't looking, so that the connection between what he says and what he does it not broken. Words were never a means to no end, because truth wasn't learned simply by listening, but by watching.

How do you know where to go, what to do, how to measure what's most important? Watch the person you trust and follow them. Like an apprentice circus performer walking the rope or juggling the dishes; you won't get it from a book. Or like Thomas Merton discovered when he asked Thich Nhat Hanh what he'd learned his first years in the monastery: "To open and close doors quietly," Thay replied. In other words, not the precepts of our texts on how to be peaceful, but how to change my life to become a peaceful person.

Francis was a great preacher, sure, because he knew how to live fully, and how to form his life around what mattered. It's like Brother Lawrence says in *The Practice of the Presence of God*: "Love increases with knowledge, and the more we know God, the more we will truly love God." But we'll never understand this if we go through life with the perspective that knowledge is gathered from the neck up. We're not observers of truth, but participants.

—

Find the story: LT 54,57
Consider a scripture: "We can touch the living Buddha. We can also touch the living Christ. When we see someone overflowing with love and understanding, someone who is keenly aware of what is going on, we know that we are very close to the Buddha and to Jesus Christ." (Thich Nhat Hanh)[84]

36 Receiving motherly love

Brotherhood and community were two of the environments of Francis' love of God. He experienced the divine surrounded by others. We rarely talk about this with him. We turn more to his preaching to birds and salving lepers' wounds—but his spiritual brothers were conduits to him of godly love more than all of the outdoors and its creatures. So for every birdbath Francis that exists I wish we had two sculptures of him with an arm around a friend. Because "Mother Earth" remains, even for someone with Francis' ability to live in the moment, a bit of an abstraction. "Mother Earth" did not care for Francis—did not envelop him—in the way another person could and did.

Francis wrote a letter to all the friars in the early days, advising those who want to live in smaller groups to organize themselves around being "mothers" and "children," taking turns caring for one another with a motherly love. There is no better way to feel God's love than this, he said.

He advised them to live in groups of four: "Two of these brothers should be 'the mother' and two, or at least one, 'the sons.' The two who are mothers should follow the life of Martha, and the sons should follow the life of Mary." Martha and Mary is a reference to the story in the New Testament Gospel of Luke where Martha busies herself with cooking and cleaning and caring for the home, when Jesus comes to visit, while Mary spends all her time with Jesus listening to his every word. Francis is saying that Mary could only do that because of Martha's care for her, and isn't that wonderful, and everyone should have such an opportunity.

There is no way to understand this motherly love as an experience of God without grasping what mystics have called the divine feminine, or the Divine Mother. The Jewish scriptures call her Sophia or Wisdom, the Mishnah calls her Shekinah, and the Hindu scriptures call her Shakti.

In the Wisdom of Solomon (a deuterocanonical book found in Catholic and Orthodox Christian bibles), Wisdom is the feminine personification of the Divine: "[I]n every generation she passes into holy souls and makes them friends of God and prophets, for God loves nothing so much as the person who lives with wisdom" (7:27).

Closer to home, and to our time, the great Black Gospel singer Marion Williams in her classic "Surely God Is Able," pounds out the lyric, "He's a mother for the motherless!" We see in Francis' life how poignantly he felt fatherless in this world, and we can surmise, given the total absence of references to his mother, also, in his life and writings, that God was Francis' Mother too.

Why a mother, specifically? Sister Joan Chittister put it very well thirty years ago: "It is precisely women's experience of God that this world lacks. A world that does not nurture its weakest, does not know God the birthing mother. A world that does not preserve the planet, does not know God the creator. A world that does not honor the spirit of compassion, does not know God the spirit. God the lawgiver, God the judge, God the omnipotent being have consumed Western spirituality and, in the end, shriveled its heart."[85]

The Indian philosopher, yogi, and poet, Sri Aurobindo

(d. 1950) taught often about the divine motherhood of God and how it is that feminine aspect of the divine that transforms people:

> It is by the constant remembrance [of her] that the being is prepared for the full opening. By the opening of the heart the Mother's presence begins to be felt and, by the opening to her Power above, the Force of the higher consciousness comes down into the body and works there to change the whole nature.[86]

Also, "she throws a spell of the intoxicating sweetness of the Divine: to be close to her is a profound happiness and to feel her within the heart is to make existence a rapture and a marvel."

This explains the joy of Saint Francis. He felt this sweetness. He was often accused of being intoxicated when he was in fact simply feeling bathed in motherly love. But he must have also known that not everyone is disposed, or given, such feelings and direct experiences. And so he instructed those who wanted to follow in his path to help each other receive this love. To be like mothers to each other. Taking turns.

—

Find the story: FW 231

Consider a scripture: "[F]or wisdom, the fashioner of all things, taught me. There is in her a spirit that is intelligent, holy, unique, manifold, subtle, agile, clear...irresistible, beneficent, humane, steadfast...all-powerful, overseeing all, and penetrating through all spirits that are intelligent, pure, and altogether subtle.... [S]he pervades and penetrates all things. For she is a breath of the power of God and a pure emanation of the glory of the Almighty.... [S]he is a reflection of eternal light, a spotless mirror of the working of God, and an image of his goodness. Although she is but one, she can do all things, and while remaining in herself, she renews all things; in every generation she passes into holy souls and makes them friends of God and prophets, for God loves nothing so much as the person who lives with wisdom. She is more beautiful than the sun and excels every constellation of the stars. Compared with the light she is found to be more radiant, for it is succeeded by the night, but against wisdom evil does not prevail. She reaches mightily from one end of the earth to the other, and she orders all things well." (Wisdom of Solomon 7:22-8:1)

Conclusion

"Live your life," my teenager says, much too often. But I'm beginning to understand.

In Zen, a teacher will remind you to stay in the present moment, to be content as a fish swimming in water and as a bird soaring through the air. It takes them almost no effort at all, because they are fully present.

I'm convinced that this is part of how and why Saint Francis loved birds and fish, looked to them as siblings, and encouraged others to love to them too. Yes, Francis' Lord said in the Gospel that we aren't to worry about tomorrow—like the birds of the air, and so on; but just as importantly I believe Francis identified with the birds' and fishes' freedom, joy, and song. They are just being themselves.

Zen also calls this having "ready mind," a mind of no attachment. My teenager might call it "going with the flow. Dude." I could use more of that, and so I'm listening and watching, learning from teachers everywhere.

Most of all, for thirty years, I've been watching and learning from Francis of Assisi, who 800 years after his passing still has much to teach us. I have written this book with the conviction—no, with the passion and desire—to experience what he experienced. I have that hope for you too.

Notes

[1] Thomas Carlyle wrote this in a letter to Ralph Waldo Emerson, July 1842.

[2] Fanny Howe, *The Needle's Eye: Passiong through Youth* (Graywolf Press, 2016), 16.

[3] Evelyn Underhill, *Mysticism: A Study in the Nature and Development of Man's Spiritual Consciousness* (Methuen, 1911), 82.

[4] Julie Seido Nelson, *Practicing Safe Zen: Navigating Pitfalls on the Road to Liberation* (Monkfish, 2025), 114.

[5] Jon Sobrino, *Christology at the Crossroads: A Latin American Approach*, trans. John Drury (Wipf & Stock, 2002), 369.

[6] Jon Sobrino. *Where Is God? Earthquake, Terrorism, Barbarity, and Hope*, trans. Margaret Wilde (Orbis Books, 2004), xx.

[7] Thoreau, *Journal*, December 30, 1853.

[8] Mary Oliver, from "When Death Comes," *New and Selected Poems, Volume One* (Beacon Press, 2005), 10. The reference in the following sentence to Brother Paul is to his beautiful memoir, *In Praise of the Useless Life* (Ave Maria Press, 2018).

[9] See John C. Wathey, *The Illusion of God's Presence: The Biological Origins of Spiritual Longing* (Prometheus, 2015), 182; and David A. Bosworth, *A House of Weeping: The Motif of Tears in Hebrew, Ugaritic, Akkadian, and Greek Prayers* (SBL Press, 2019), 11.

[10] Howard Thurman, *For the Inward Journey: The Writings of Howard Thurman*, selected by Anne Spencer Thurman (Friends United Press: 1984), 259.

[11] *Zen Mind, Beginner's Mind: Informal Talks on Zen Meditation and Practice*, ed. T. Dixon (Shambhala, 2011).

[12] Helene Cixous, *Stigmata: Escaping Texts*, trans. Eric Prenowitz (Routledge, 2005), 201.

[13] Francis, *Francis of Assisi: Early Documents, Volume 1*, eds. Regis J. Armstrong, OFM Cap, J.A. Wayne Hellmann, OFM Conv., and William J. Short, OFM (New City Press, 1999), 57.

[14] Ibid., 75, 89.

[15] Thich Nhat Hahn, *Anger: Wisdom for Cooling the Flames* (Riverhead, 2002), 22.

[16] This is Andre Louf OCSO's phrase, from *The Way of the Heart: The Spiritual Experience of Andre Louf*, by Charles Wright, trans. Brian Kerns OCSO (Cistercian Publications, 2024), xxiii.

[17] *850 Sayings of the Baal Shem Tov*, trans. Rabbi Zev Wineberg (ind. pub., 2020), 27.

[18] Thomas of Celano, from "The Legend for Use in the Choir," ca. 1230, in *Francis of Assisi: Early Documents, Vol. 1*, 320.

[19] Thich Nhat Hanh, *In Love and Trust: Letters from a Zen Master* (Parallax Press, 2024), 243-44.

[20] I've written about this in several books, but I recently appreciated how a reviewer in the *TLS* put it at the start of a review of Volker Leppin's new biography of Francis: "Even as capitalism was showing its first timid signs of life in medieval Europe, a series of vigorous counter-movements began to undermine it.... Although medieval anticapitalism didn't have a Karl Marx, it arguably had even more formidable opponents.... above all, St. Francis of Assisi." Costica Bradatan, "A life like a poem," *The Times Literary Supplement*, February 7, 2025; 5.

[21] Julie Seido Nelson, *Practicing Safe Zen*, 10-11.

[22] Richard Rohr, *The Tears of Things: Prophetic Wisdom for an Age of Outrage* (Convergent, 2025), 53.

[23] Translation of Joseph P. Amar in *Syriac Christian Culture: Beginnings to Renaissance*, eds. Aaron Michael Butts and Robin Darling Young (CUA Press, 2020), 26.

[24] Henri J.M. Nouwen, *Spiritual Direction: Wisdom for the Long Walk of Faith* (HarperOne, 2015), 5.
[25] Teresa of Avila, *The Life of Teresa of Jesus: The Autobiography of Teresa of Avila*, ed. and trans. E. Allison Peers (Doubleday, 1960), 166.
[26] Nouwen, *Spiritual Direction*, 18.
[27] Joseph Campbell, *Thou Art That: Transforming Religious Metaphor* (New World Library, 2013), 112-13.
[28] Lyanda Lynn Haupt, *Mozart's Starling* (Back Bay Books, 2018), 8.
[29] Netta Weinstein, Heather Hansen, and Thuy-vy T. Nguyen, *Solitude: The Science and Power of Being Alone* (Cambridge University Press, 2024), 53.
[30] George Pattison, *A Philosophy of Prayer: Nothingness, Language, and Hope* (Fordham University Press, 2024), 8-9.
[31] Quoted by Gerry Shishin Wick in his *The Five Ranks of Zen: Tozan's Path of Being, Nonbeing and Compassion* (Shambhala, 2024), 18.
[32] Quoted in *Gardens of Awakening: A Guide to the Aesthetics, History, and Spirituality of Kyoto's Zen Landscapes*, Kazuaki Tanahashi (Shambhala, 2024), 43.
[33] See "The Three Tenets" at Zenpeacemakers.org.
[34] Friedrich Nietzsche essentially said this, although I hestitate to quote him outright in the text for fear that you'll think I'm mad. See *Dawn: Thoughts on the Presumptions of Morality*, trans. Brittain Smith (Stanford University Press, 2011), section 14.
[35] Czeslaw Milosz, *The Witness of Poetry* (Harvard University Press, 1984), 99.
[36] This story comes from Les Kaye, *I Had a Good Teacher: Practicing Suzuki Roshi's Way of Zen* (Monkfish, 2025), x.
[37] "All Things Pray," by Micah Joseph Berdichevski, trans. Aaron Ofer, in *Siddur Sha'ar Zahav* (Congregation Sha'ar Zahav, San Francisco, CA, 2009), 215.
[38] Jacob Riyeff, *Be Radiant: A Sonata Pome* (Fernwood Press, 2024), 15.

[39] See The Infancy Gospel of Thomas in *Apocryphal Gospels*, trans. Simon Gathercole (Penguin, 2021), 31-32.

[40] Thoreau, from his essay, "Walking."

[41] Teilhard de Chardin, "The Mass on the World" in *The Heart of Matter*, trans. Rene Hague (Harvest/HBJ, 1980), 119-20.

[42] George Prochnik, *In Pursuit of Silence: Listening for Meaning in a World of Noise* (Anchor, 2011), 293.

[43] (Weatherhill, 1970), 47. Perhaps to reinforce the point, Suzuki Roshi said, according to his biographer David Chadwick, when presented with a first copy of his book, "Good book. I didn't write it, but it looks like a good book." *(Crooked Cucumber: The Life and Zen Teachings of Shunryu Suzuki*, Broadway Books, 1999, 352.)

[44] Abraham Joshua Heschel, *The Sabbath: Its Meaning for Modern Man* (Farrar, Straus and Giroux, 1951), 14, 28.

[45] Bonaventure, from the prologue of *Itinerarium Mentis in Deum*; see *Into God*, 9. The second, longer quotation from Bonaventure in this chapter comes also from page 9.

[46] Holly Hillgardner, *Longing and Letting Go: Christian and Hindu Practices of Passionate Non-attachment* (Oxford University Press, 2016), 72-73.

[47] See https://ronrolheiser.com/inchoate-desire/.

[48] Chief Yellow Lark and Chief Red Cloud, "Prayer of Chief Yellow Lark, n.d." (2020). *Miscellaneous.* 21. https://nwcommons.nwciowa.edu/lecocqmiscellaneous/21.

[49] Thomas Merton, letter, *The Hidden Ground of Love: The Letters of Thomas Merton on Religious Experience and Social Concerns*, ed. William H. Shannon (Harcourt, 1993), 473.

[50] *Three Treatises on the Divine Images*, trans. Andrew Louth (St. Vladimir's Seminary Press, 2003), 29.

[51] Chloe Dalton, *Raising Hare: A Memoir* (Pantheon Books, 2024), 274-75.

[52] *Bhakti Yoga: Tales and Teachings from the Bhagavata Purana*, trans. Edwin F. Bryant (North Point Press, 2017), 476.

[53] Linda M. Paterson, *The Troubadours* (Reaktion Books, 2024), 9.

[54] See Steven E. Turley, *Franciscan Spirituality and Mission in New Spain, 1524-1599* (Routledge, 2024), 5-8.

[55] Yuria Celidwen, *Flourishing Kin: Indigenous Wisdom for Collective Well-Being* (Sounds True, 2024), 199.

[56] Jacques de Vitry, in *Francis of Assisi: Early Documents, Vol. 1*, 584.

[57] See Wendell Berry, *What Are People For? Essays* (Counterpoint, 2010).

[58] Mary Oliver, from the poem "Messenger," from *Thirst* (Beacon Press, 2007), 1.

[59] Trans. D.T. Suzuki, *Manual of Zen Buddhism* (Rider, 1950), 14.

[60] Thomas Merton, *New Seeds of Contemplation* (New Directions, 2007), 21.

[61] Merton, *New Seeds of Contemplation*, 30.

[62] From *To Shine One Corner of the World*, ed. David Chadwick (Broadway Books, 2001), 43.

[63] Quoted in Richard Ellmann, *James Joyce* (Oxford University Press, 1982), 664.

[64] *The Gospel of Sri Ramakrishna*, trans. Swami Nikhilananda (Ramakrishna-Vivekananda Center, 2000), 122.

[65] Thomas Merton, *Zen and the Birds of Appetite* (New Directions, 1968), 111.

[66] Shunryu Suzuki, *Branching Streams Flow in the Darkness: Zen Talks on the Sandokai*, eds. Mel Weitsman and Michael Wenger (University of California Press, 2001), 28-29.

[67] From "A Community of Spirit," trans. Coleman Barks et al, in *The Essential Rumi: New Expanded Edition* (HarperOne, 2004), 3.

[68] Byung-Chul Han, *The Spirit of Hope*, trans. Daniel Steuer (Polity, 2024), 65.

[69] Albert Einstein, quoted in *Life* magazine, May 2, 1955, 64.

[70] Rabbi Adina Allen, "The Art of Teshuvah," at MyJewishLearning.org, accessed January 10, 2025. https://www.myjewishlearning.com/article/the-art-of-teshuvah/

[71] Anne Frank, *The Diary of a Young Girl*, trans. B.M. Mooyaart-Doubleday (Bantam, 1993), July 6, 1944.

[72] From *The Road to Assisi* in *The Complete Francis of Assisi*, ed. Sweeney (Paraclete Press, 2015), 38.

[73] Martha Nussbaum, *Upheavals of Thought: The Intelligence of Emotions* (Cambridge University Press, 2001). See also Bosworth, *A House of Weeping*, 11-13.

[74] Thich Nhat Hanh, *The Path of Emancipation: Talks from a 21-Day Mindfulness Retreat* (Parallax Press, 2000), x.

[75] See David Burr, *The Spiritual Franciscans: From Protest to Persecution in the Century After Saint Francis* (Pennsylvania State University Press, 2001), 274-77.

[76] Pablo d'Ors, *Biography of Silence: An Essay on Meditation*, trans. David Shook (Parallax Press, 2018), 22-23.

[77] Les Kaye, chapter 10 of *I Had a Good Teacher*; David Chadwick, *Crooked Cucumber*, xii; David Chadwick, *Tassajara Stories: A Sort of Memoir/Oral History of the First Zen Buddhist Monastery in the West—The First Year—1967* (Monkfish, 2025), 27.

[78] Evelyn Underhill, *The Fruits of the Spirit, Light of Christ, Abba* (David McKay Co., 1956), from "Abba," 1. (This book does not have continuous pagination.)

[79] This is a paraphrase by G. Geltner from his *The Making of Medieval Antifraternalism: Polemic, Violence, Deviance, and Remembrance* (Oxford University Press, 2012), 23 (quote), 19.

[80] I wrote about all of this in detail in *The Enthusiast: How the Best Friend of Francis of Assisi Almost Destroyed What He Started* (Ave Maria Press, 2016).

[81] Thomas Merton, *Dancing in the Water of Life: Seeking Peace in the Hermitage (The Journals of Thomas Merton Vol. 5 1963-1965)* (HarperOne, 1998), 327.

[82] Shunryu Suzuki, from "Nirvana, the Waterfall," in *Zen Mind, Beginner's Mind*, 94.

[83] Kabir, in Rabindranath Tagore's translation, *One Hundred Poems of Kabir* (Macmillan, 1962), XL, 47.
[84] *Living Buddha Living Christ: 20th Anniversary Edition* (Riverhead, 2007), 58.
[85] Joan D. Chittister, *Heart of Flesh: Feminist Spirituality for Women and Men* (Eerdmans, 1998), 5.
[86] Sri Aurobindo, *The Mother, with Letters on the Mother and Translations of Prayers and Meditations* (Sri Aurobindo Ashram, 1972), 127. The quote that follows is from pages 30-31.

Acknowledgments

Thank you to Brother Mark Joseph Costello, OFM Cap, provincial minister of the Capuchin Province of St. Joseph, for the invitation to give a retreat to his brothers in spring 2024, when some of these practices were first discussed. Thank you to Sister Phyllis Wirtz, of the School Sisters of Saint Francis, for invitations to address their community, which have also been helpful to me in conceiving how this project might come together.

A portion of these teachings appeared in my e-course on the spiritual experiences of Saint Francis at SpiritualityandPractice.com in the autumn of 2025. Thank you to Mary Ann and Frederic Brussat for the invitation to teach it, and to Monkfish Book Publishing for permission to preview some of these teachings there.

Thank you to James Martin, SJ, Kaira Jewel Lingo, Rabbi Or Rose, and Karen Kiefer for previewing the manuscript and offering such generous comments for marketing.

The reader will see that my sources are many and varied, but I feel the need to point in particular to Thich Nhat Hanh, from whom I feel I've learned much about the spirit of Saint Francis in the past several years. This book quotes Thay more than any I've written before.

A special thank you to Brother Thomas Skowron, OFM Cap, for the drawing you see in the frontispiece.

About the Author

Jon M. Sweeney is an award-winning author and independent scholar who has been interviewed by the *Dallas Morning News* and *The Irish Catholic*, on radio with NPR and the BBC, and on television at CBS Saturday Morning. He's a rare author found in scholarly journals as well as Romper.com and *Catster Magazine*.

Jon's books on Franciscan spirituality have sold a quarter million copies. He's also the author of thirty books on spirituality, mysticism, biography, and memoir including *Meister Eckhart's Book of the Heart*, coauthored with Mark S. Burrows, *Thomas Merton: An Introduction to His Life and Practices*; and *Sit in the Sun: And Other Lessons in the Wisdom of Cats*. His medieval history, *The Pope Who Quit*, was optioned by HBO.

Today Jon works in book publishing as a partner at Monkfish Book Publishing, editor of *Living City* magazine, and contributing editor for books at SpiritualityandPractice.com. He speaks at literary and religious conferences, in churches, retreat centers, and independent bookstores. He's a Roman Catholic married to a rabbi; their interfaith marriage has been profiled in national media. He lives with his wife, daughter, and animals in a little house facing the Green Mountains just outside Middlebury, Vermont.